WRITERS AND THEIR WORK

ISOBEL ARMSTRONG
General Editor

BRYAN LOUGHREY
Advisory Editor

JOHN BETJEMAN

SIR JOHN BETJEMAN

Sir John Betjeman unveils a plaque to W. H. Auden in Poets' Corner, Westminster Abbey, 1974.

JOHN
BETJEMAN

DENNIS BROWN

Northcote House
in association with the
British Council

© Copyright 1999 by Dennis Brown

First published in 1999 by Northcote House Publishers Ltd, Plymbridge House, Estover Road, Plymouth PL6 7PY, United Kingdom.
Tel: +44 (01752) 202368 Fax: +44 (01752) 202330.

British Library Cataloguing-in-Publication Data
A catalogue record for this book is available from the British Library

ISBN 0-7463-0895-7

Typeset by PDQ Typesetting, Newcastle-under-Lyme
Printed and bound in the United Kingdom

To the memory of my father, Ernest Stuart Brown, and his Valdepeñas 'conventicle', and for my grandchildren – Jessica, Emma, and Jacob

Contents

Acknowledgements

To John Murray (Publishers) Ltd for permission to quote from Sir John Betjeman's poems, as referenced, and to Deborah Gill for facilitating this. To John Mole for permission to quote, as epigraph, from his *Selected Poems*, and for reading and commenting on chapters as they were written. To Bryan Loughrey for commissioning this work, Brian Hulme for his encouraging telephonic advice, Patrick Grant for his 'transatlantic' support, George Wotton for some very apt comments on Chapter 2, Eibhlín Evans for help with the Select Bibliography, John Heald, Honorary Secretary of the Betjeman Society, for some important factual information and his Betjemanian enthusiasm, and Sharon Monteith and Nahem Yousaf for their unfailing interest. Lastly, yet again, to my wife, Sam, for her formatting skills and maintaining a loving environment that makes such work possible. Last of all, but not least, *Deo Gratias*.

Biographical Outline

1906   John Betjeman(n) born on 28 August at 52 Parliament Hill Mansions, London NW5.

1909   The Betjemann family move to 31 West Hill, Highgate N6.

1911   Begins formal schooling at Byron House.

1915   Enters Highgate Junior School in September and remains until March 1917. During this time he writes a poem about Zeppelin raids.

1916   Gives *The Best of Betjeman* to 'the American Master', T. S. Eliot.

1917   In May goes as a boarder to the Dragon School, Oxford. While there begins to explore the city and nearby villages. Meanwhile, the family home becomes relocated in Church Street, Chelsea. Summer holidays are still regularly spent at the family cottage in Cornwall.

1920   Goes to Marlborough College in September. Among his fellow-pupils are Anthony Blunt and Louis MacNeice.

1924   On St Valentine's Day *The Heretick* (a Marlburian review) is published with a poem by Betjeman in it – followed by another poem, 'Ye Olde Cottage', in the June issue. Also contributes to the *Marlburian*, the school magazine. Corresponds with Lord Alfred Douglas (Oscar Wilde's 'Bosie') until forbidden to by his father.

1925   Goes to Magdalen College, Oxford, in the Michaelmas term. His tutor in English Language and Literature is C. S. Lewis – neither appreciated the qualities of the other. His many acquaintances at Oxford are celebrated later in *Summoned by Bells* – they included W. H. Auden and Evelyn Waugh.

1926   Contributes his first poem to the *Isis*. Visits Pierce

Synnott's country house in Ireland, and also Sezincote in Gloucestershire.

1927   Provides architectural notes to the *Cherwell,* and then becomes editor as well as contributor. Edward James subsidizes the review and then, in turn, becomes editor.

1928   Having failed his Divinity examination, Betjeman leaves Oxford. Returns, but is then sent down. However, he retains contacts with Oxford friends and literary magazines.

1929   Becomes private secretary to Sir Horace Plunkett, the politician, but is dismissed within two months. Secures a school-teaching post at Heddon Court, East Barnet.

1930   Writes articles for, and begins work at, the *Architectural Review,* and helps promote modernist styles from Charles Rennie Mackintosh to Le Corbusier as well as Victorian work.

1931   Becomes engaged to Camilla Sykes, but then is romantically attracted to both Pamela Mitford and Penelope Chetwode. *Mount Zion* printed privately by Edward James.

1932   Develops ideas for a Shell Guide series.

1933   Marries Penelope Chetwode at Edmonton Register Office on 29 July.

1934   Edits the Shell Guide, *Cornwall Illustrated.*

1934–5 Becomes film critic for the *Evening Standard,* but leaves after a few months.

1935–9 Working in the Shell department of publicity.

1936   Edits the Shell Guide, *Devon.*

1937   John Murray brings out *Continual Dew,* Betjeman's second collection.

1939   Works for the Films Division of the Ministry of Information after the start of the Second World War.

1940   Publication of *Old Lights for New Chancels.*

1941–3 Becomes United Kingdom Press Attaché (with secret Admiralty work later) in neutral Dublin. The IRA seeks to assassinate him as a British spy.

1945   Publication of *New Bats in Old Belfries.* After the war, Betjeman publishes several topographic books and does journalist work for various newspapers.

1954   Publication of *A Few Late Chrysanthemums.*

1958   Publication of *Collected Poems.* They achieve enormous

	success in terms of sales and popularity.
1960	Publication of *Summoned by Bells*, Betjeman's autobiography in blank verse. Awarded the Queen's Medal for poetry and the CBE (Companion, Order of the British Empire).
1962	Begins his series of television films about towns in the West Country. Such films continue until 1964. Publication of *A Ring of Bells*.
1966	Publication of *High and Low*.
1968	Made Companion of Literature, Royal Society of Literature.
1969	Awarded a Knighthood.
1972	Appointed Poet Laureate.
1973	Made Honorary Member of the American Academy of Arts and Letters.
1974	Publication of *A Nip in the Air*. Declaims 'Inland Waterway' in the presence of the Queen Mother at the opening of the Upper Avon, Stratford, 1 June.
1983	Public appearance to name British Rail locomotive no. 86229 'Sir John Betjeman'.
1984	Dies, following the onset of Parkinson's Disease and suffering several strokes. Is buried at St Enodoc Church, Cornwall.

Abbreviations

BB   *The Best of Betjeman*, selected by John Guest (London: Penguin in association with John Murray, 1978)

CP   *Collected Poems*, compiled with an introduction by the Earl of Birkenhead (London: John Murray, 1997)

LI   *John Betjeman: Letters Volume One 1926 to 1951*, edited by Candida Lycett Green (London: John Murray, 1994)

SBB   *Summoned by Bells* (London: John Murray, 1992)

transfigured, translated,
A fiend in the cloud of his fierce adoration.
(John Mole, 'John Betjeman writes the William Blake Poem')

Introduction

Sir John Betjeman (1906–84) remains, surely, the most popular of 'contemporary' British poets. That is, I believe, a fact worth taking seriously in a democratic society. In his lifetime, Betjeman became a representative figure for the many who feel that poetry should be readily understandable, rooted in common perceptions, and formal in rhythm and rhyme. In this regard, he became not only the most accepted Poet Laureate since Tennyson but also a prolific radio and television 'Personality'.

However, Betjeman the public figure, and even Betjeman the architectural and cultural commentator, should not obscure for readers his true vocation and commitment. John Betjeman was first and last a poet. And he was recognized as this by such contrastive poetic figures as T. S. Eliot, W. H. Auden, and Philip Larkin. The comparative lack of academic-critical interest in his work thus reflects more on the pretensions of criticism and literary theory than on the quality of Betjeman's contribution.

This introductory book – written for general readers as much as for students – will be focused on Betjeman's poetry itself: any critical or theoretical comment will emerge out of an attentive consideration of the poems. 'I was a poet,' Betjeman asserts, concerning a youthful failure to shoot rabbits in *Summoned by Bells* (*SBB* 21). This short study takes the poet at his own estimation.

For this reason, the biographical sketch, text, and bibliography are primarily concerned with Betjeman's poetic career. No doubt Bevis Hillier's definitive biography will be completed soon. But the poetry will remain the chief reason why such books will be of particular interest. And, as Chapter 1 indicates, the popularity of Betjeman's poems has much to do with his willingness to confine his writing to conventional verse forms

1

that remain the generally accepted norm of English poetic practice.

At the same time, the poet was content to employ wit, compassion, and common sense rather than furthering the intellectuality, austerity, and satiric extremism that Modernism had pioneered. Betjeman's basic style represents a different kind of *rappel à l'ordre* – begun in the wildly politicized 1930s; and it set a precedent in the 1940s for the coming emphases of the Movement from the 1950s onwards, themselves, no doubt, an English 'empirical' reaction, rooted in Second World War isolation, to European left-wing posturing (Brecht, Sartre, Althusser, and so on) as the cold war became consolidated.

Betjeman's traditional aesthetic and socio-political common sense have not commended his work to either New Critical or New Left cultural commentators. But, for all its middle-class values, Betjeman's writing represents what most people mean by poetry, when they think of it at all. 'Poetry Day' polls in the 1990s have indicated that Betjeman remains a 'classic' along with such as Wordsworth, Tennyson, Kipling, de la Mare, and Larkin.

Further, Betjeman's poetry has come to represent a widely accepted version of England and Englishness that may well become strengthened as devolution, accompanied by 'Celtic' cultural chauvinisms takes hold. In Chapter 3 I consider how Englishness in Betjeman's poetry is constructed in terms of 'place-myth' based on topographical evocation. And, while the poet's television persona may have conveyed a somewhat 'old-world' image, his poems are quite fully in tune with a postmodern interest in environmentalism, conservation, and communitarianism.

Betjeman's Englishness, in fact, always constituted a kind of 'Third Way' – despite the radicalism of some of his early friends, the conservatism of many of his later admirers. In this Betjeman's Anglicanism is important – discussed in my last chapter. The Anglican middle way represents the spiritual basis of what has been hailed as the 'Third Way'. It constitutes an ongoing strand in British thought – close, but in religious mode, to Orwell's secular 'decency'. While the Right still invoke 'Victorian values' and the Left still commend to us the farcical *Guignol* of 'Paris 1968', Betjeman's 'Third Way' anticipates the central temper of contemporary thinking.

2

Betjeman's verse is also relevant to a growing intellectual interest in 'masculinities' as Chapter 2 suggests. *Summoned by Bells*, in particular, is one of the few 'contemporary' longer poems that explores male acculturation from 'within'. I feel that this aspect makes the poem far more than a narrative of sly social climbing. The poet's psychological middle way appears to have been the product of a successful negotiation between his father's robustness and his mother's sentiment – resulting in Betjeman's admiration for honest construction (whether of furniture, churches, or automobiles) on the one hand, on the other his empathy (with the exploited, the saddened, or the dying).

Similarly, the poet's more mature negotiation between late Modernism (at the *Architectural Review*) and the Victorian Arts and Crafts movement led to his idiosyncratic poetic contribution – where prospectively postmodern themes come 'encase'd in traditional forms – especially, as we shall see, the basic quatrain. Overall, Betjeman's styled masculinity – formed in the First World War, tempered in the Second – was struggled for, achieved, and perfected. He became one of the most unique, distinctive, and lovable of twentieth-century poets. And his wide readership surely endorses this view.

Yet his style – as both man and poet – was consolidated early and expanded rather than much developed. For this reason I have not followed the normal procedure for this kind of introductory book – to trace, through chronologically based chapters, the 'evolution' of a writer's work. Rather, the chapter plan is based on important interconnecting facets of Betjeman's work as a whole – four 'essays' based on: (1) a strategy of verse-'containment'; (2) an exploration of a certain kind of masculinity; (3) a construction of Englishness through place-myth; and (4) a deployment of well-tempered spirituality.

Throughout, the aim is to emphasize, through the discussion of specific poems considered under a particular theme, the special status of Betjeman's contribution – and its relevance to contemporary social conditions, poetics, and literary theory. Betjeman's poetry remains loved; but his reputation has been patronized by literary critics for far too long. I would wish to show, in this book, how relevance and pleasure come united in John Betjeman's complete poetic *œuvre*.

1

To Encase in Rhythm and Rhyme

> Miss J. Hunter Dunn, Miss J. Hunter Dunn,
> Furnish'd and burnish'd by Aldershot sun...
>
> (CP 87)

These words at the beginning of 'A Subaltern's Love Song' (or 'Love-song', 'Contents' (1958)) are probably the best known of all John Betjeman's well-loved lines. I had them by heart at the age of 13 after a single reading of the poem. Although the poem spoke of a social world quite unfamiliar to me (and I had no idea what a 'Subaltern' was), the rhythm and rhyme fixed themselves in my mind. Were the first lines composed on one of those steam-train journeys the poet so savoured? *Miss-J.-Hun-ter-Dunn* – wasn't that how those hissing, panting, clanking locomotives got under way, before slowly developing an even rhythm – 'Furnish'd and burnish'd by Aldershot sun'? And then there was the rhyme, prepared for and arrived at as an echo – exact, witty, haunting. The quatrain form, too, was compelling – a staple of the Victorian poets and the hymn-writers Betjeman loved, but around 1920 employed by the writer of another famous 'Love Song', Betjeman's 'American master' T. S. Eliot, to devastating ironic effect when 'Sweeney' became 'agonised'.[1] Betjeman's own usage of the quatrain is familiar, humorous, and reassuring. A quirky, fantasizing story gets told, through controlled sound patterns, to alight on an idealized sense of an ending: 'And now I'm engaged to Miss Joan Hunter Dunn' – a consummation as devoutly to be wished as the closure of a Romantic ode ('And gathering swallows...') or a Victorian novel ('Reader, I married him').

4

In a century that has restlessly destabilized the formal poetic line (Imagism, *The Waste Land*, the *Cantos*, Ted Hughes's *Crow*, the 'L=A=N=G=U=A=G=E' experimenters...), Betjeman's work has consistently held to traditional boundaries, as if these constituted the essence of poetic Englishness. And, although his stanzaic forms have varied considerably, the quatrain appears to be the poet's core aesthetic shape. If four sections of the 'Sir John Piers' sequence are counted separately, I find around fifty quatrains in the 1958 *Collected Poems* – about a third of the total. Most typically, Betjeman uses the rhyme scheme ABAB – more normative than AABB, which utilizes the ironic possibilities of the couplet (as in 'A Subaltern's Love Song'), or ABBA, which *In Memoriam* rendered the 'bell-toll' of literary mourning. Yet quite frequently in Betjeman's quatrains only the second and fourth lines are rhymed, as in 'Undenominational' (whose title and first line surely replicate 'Polyphiloprogenitive' in 'Mr Eliot's Sunday Morning Service'). The poem ends:

> Revival ran along the hedge
> And made my spirit whole
> When steam was on the window panes
> And glory in my soul.
>
> (CP 28)

Rhyme is a telling device in the poet's work, but not the fetish it is for some – and *Summoned by Bells*, for instance, is mainly in unrhymed blank verse. Basically, Betjeman's instinct was to deploy the central forms of English verse, especially those bequeathed by the Victorians, and to do everything decently and in order.

Betjeman was neither unaware of modernist verse experimentation nor ignorant of literary critical views of his time – the *Scrutiny* group are surely alluded to ('blow the lamps out') in the section of his verse autobiography which indicates his method:

> My urge was to encase in rhythm and rhyme
> The things I saw and felt (I could not *think*).
>
> (SBB 17)

The word 'encase' is worth dwelling on. It recalls Romantic antecedents, such as Wordsworth's 'Cased in the unfeeling armour of old time' ('Elegiac Stanzas...Peele Castle'), or even

Keats's 'magic casements' – but suggests as much, perhaps, the artisan skills of the family firm the poet rejected: the Betjemann & Sons 'Tantalus', for instance, 'encased' decanters of spirits. The poet has elsewhere elaborated on his employment of 'ear, conciseness and clarity': 'Ear is only gained by reading and re-reading the ancient models who appeal to you. For me that means Tennyson...Keep the same attitude of soul throughout the poem' (*LI* 432). Clearly Betjeman's aim was not Pound's Imagist 'natural cadence', nor did he wish to 'break the pentameter'. For him, 'individual talent' should work within a formal 'tradition': it was not metre and rhyme schemes that should be made new. However, the poet's placement within the overall 'modern movement' is more problematic than his reputation has allowed. Just as the advocate of Victorian ecclesiastical architecture was one of the first commentators to bring the work of Le Corbusier before the British public, so his first volume of poems was published by a patron of Surrealist art (Edward James) and his second, *Continual Dew*, had a Surreal cover-design with a hand sprouting leaves.[2] The work is not merely 'antiquarian'. While the Betjeman poetic line retains formality (as did Philip Larkin's in the 1950s or Glyn Maxwell's in the early l990s), the subject matter is not only of the 'modern' world but prefigures postmodern concerns such as environmentalism, communitarianism, the 'hyperreality' of consumer icons, and a return of the spiritual repressed. In general, Betjeman's work emphasizes that, while in poetry, as in science, there are 'paradigm shifts' from time to time, the 'normal' work is one of assimilation and elaboration.[3]

To 'encase' in poetic words is ultimately, I suggest, to exercise psychic control. This is put another way in 'Sunday Morning, King's Cambridge': 'To praise Eternity contained in Time and coloured glass' (*CP* 152) – 'encase'-ment as visual art. 'Contained', here, is a suggestive word – and one that, independently, has been given both prominence and resonance in recent British School psychoanalysis. Wilfred Bion, hero of the First World War, pupil of Melanie Klein, psychoanalyst of Samuel Beckett, and originator of psychoanalytic group work in the Second World War, outlines this usage of the term in *Attention and Interpretation* (1983): 'According to his background a patient will describe various objects as containers, such as his mind, the unconscious, the nation; others as contained, such as his money, his ideas.'[4] In *The Good Society and the Inner World* (1991), the sociologist Michael Rustin has expanded the idea of 'containment' to include structures in the public domain:

> Cultural forms are one mode of containment and facilitation for...growth, throughout life, and their availability to all as living forms is therefore central to the possibility of a good society...Our experience in responding to cultural forms (as well as that of making them) derives from inner unconscious experience and its symbolization...An educational conclusion which can be drawn from the relevance of psychoanalysis is that it is necessary to create learning settings which give space to the experience of feeling as a primary element of understanding.[5]

My suggestion here is simple. Poetic form constitutes such a 'mode of containment' or 'learning setting'. And this can hold true both for the poet ('making them') and the appreciative reader ('experience in responding'). In fact, the more readily acceptable the poetic form, the more easily will less sophisticated readers identify with it. Most readers prefer traditional forms – forms that ultimately reach back to the oral realm of rote recitation, song, or hymn. For instance, the formal shaping of nursery rhymes says a great deal about where the 'common reader' is coming from:

> Humpty Dumpty sat on a wall,
> Humpty Dumpty had a great fall...
>
> Hickory, Dickory, dock,
> The mouse ran up the clock...

Let us compare the containing power of such couplets with some lines published in the *London Review of Books*, in this week of writing, by John Ashbery (a poet I much admire):

> Outside, life prattles on merrily,
> like an embroidered towel, and would probably be too weak to object
> if we decided to postpone the picnic until November.
> I hear you; the arches under the embankment
> are part of what I'm all about. I too was weaned from excess
> in some silvery age now lost in a blizzard of envelopes...

> ('The Village of Sleep')[6]

Such free-verse lines also constitute a 'mode of containment', a 'learning setting'; but they are looser, more leisurely, and more 'literary' (a knowledge of, say, Walt Whitman, Eliot, and Wallace Stevens helps considerably). They evidence a far greater willingness to enquire into and develop disparate modes of experience and expression than the average formal poem. But the mode of containment here is more like clingfilm than (as Keats put it) swaying about on the 'rocking horse' of the metrical couplet – or conforming to the quadrille of the quatrain.

I am interested in placing rather than judging. Briefly, Betjeman's mode of containment ('to encase') is founded upon traditional (finally oral) modes of linguistic communication which feel safe for poet and reader alike – and this allows for a comfort structure (a kind of verse teddy bear), even when the content is disturbing. Here is the first verse in the *Collected Poems*:

> She died in the upstairs bedroom
> By the light of the ev'ning star
> That shone through the plate glass window
> From over Leamington Spa.

('Death in Leamington' (CP 1))

The subject matter of this poem is bleak, claustrophobic, even funereal. Yet the formal 'container' ('star'...'Spa') provides a means of rendering the theme aesthetically tolerable and, in odd ways, pleasurable. In many poems, Betjeman (like Philip Larkin later) relies on rhythm and rhyme to transform emotional 'drowning' into poetic 'waving':

> And say shall I groan in dying,
> As I twist the sweaty sheet?
> Or gasp for breath uncrying,
> as I feel my senses drown'd
> While the air is swimming with insects
> and children play in the street?

('The Cottage Hospital' (CP 179))

The phenomenon of encasement, or 'containment', can be demonstrated in the unit of the individual line. Indeed, the poetic line is the ultimate verse-container and precisely what sets poetry off from the ubiquitous realm of informational prose. Betjeman's line is typically clear, forthright, and regular, frequently relying on three or four bold stresses:

> She let the blinds unroll.
>
> ('Death in Leamington' (*CP* 1))

or:

> The Pooters walked to Watney Lodge.
>
> ('Thoughts on "The Diary of a Nobody"' (*CP* 218))

Basically, Betjeman's lines utilize a 'balladic' tradition rather than the 'high' style of the sonnet, epic, or formal ode. English iambic cadence (short/long) is the norm, although there are plenty of attractive variations – for example, 'Rumbling under blackened girders, Midland, bound for Cricklewood' ('Parliament Hill Fields' (*CP* 85)). The Betjeman line endorses popular preference over 'canonical' sonorities – the kind of form Auden adopted in poems such as 'Miss Gee'. As Geoffrey Grigson once put it:

> part of what ambiguous John Betjeman intends is this: that in spite of Eliot and Herbert Read [odd pairing!], we and he should *feel at home*, should feel ourselves, by the sound and the properties, back by the loose-cover of the armchair, by which, in 1909, we learnt ' *Up the airy mountain, down the rushy glen*'.[7]

However, date snobbery (1909) is scarcely the issue here. More to the point is that the poet (however ideologically situated) is an exponent of populist poetics – even when his subject matter is 'campily' middle class. In his controversial book *Poetry as Discourse* (1983), Antony Easthope has interesting things to say about the 'naturalized' pentameter form, Englishness, and the demotic as opposed to 'courtly' (or 'high') verse:

> Beside iambic pentameter there is the older accentual four-stress metre inherited from Old English poetry. While the pentameter, conventionally defined as a line of ten syllables alternately unstressed and stressed, legislates for both stress and syllable, accentual metre requires only that the line should contain four stressed syllables and says nothing about the unstressed syllables. Since stress or syllable prominence is phonetically much more significant in English than syllable duration, accentual metre has a strong claim to be more natural in Old, Middle and Modern English.[8]

Easthope goes on to quote Northrop Frye's view that 'four-stress line seems to be inherent' in the language, and is 'the common rhythm of popular poetry in all periods, of ballads and most nursery rhymes'. While Betjeman's overall practice somewhat straddles the polarity set up between 'pentameter' and 'four-stress', iambic and unstressed syllables, it is clear that the core of his work adheres to the more populist, older and oral model. This becomes interesting in terms of Easthope's apparent drawing up of class lines: 'The two forms – ballad and the Renaissance courtly poem – exemplify opposed kinds of discourse: one collective, popular, intersubjective, accepting the text as a poem to be performed; the other individualistic, elitist, privatized, offering the text as representation of a voice speaking.'[9] Betjeman's poetry is essentially to be 'performed' – and it does not necessarily require his own, rather plummy, accent.

Here I am less interested in social placement than the use of the 'balladic' line as a psycholinguistic mode of 'containment'. Rhythmic 'encase'-ment becomes a form of control and hence a comfort mechanism, as in the following random selection of lines:

> Far-surrounding, seem their own.
>
> ('Upper Lambourne' (CP 44))

> Ringleader, tom-boy, and chum to the weak.
>
> ('Myfanwy' (CP 70))

> And lightly skims the midge.
>
> ('Henley on Thames' (CP 84))

> Are those we take for granted.
>
> ('The Hon. Sec.' (CP 272))

The above are all ending lines; they demonstrate, in that important position, the inner dynamic of Betjeman's lines in general – what in 'Bristol', in relation to populist bellringing, he called 'mathematic pattern' (CP 89). Put another way, Betjeman's best-known poems conform to the conventions of song writing, as well as hymn writing; they could easily be set to either 'classic' or 'pop' music. This says a lot about their cultural placement. The individual line is to appeal to the common ear for rhythmic ordering and euphony. Other poetic devices – diction, imagery, syntactical subtlety, symbolism, or any type of ambiguity – are subordinate to the requirements of stressed rhythm and assonance. In this, the lines accord with heartbeat, breathing, and walking regularities. The psychic 'containment' is rooted in ultimately physiological phenomena. So the poems communicate a shaping of experience into simply, but cannily, ordered words. Or, as Theodore Roethke fondly wrote: 'The shapes a bright container can contain.'

The poet's friend John Sparrow is on record as suggesting that the reading of Betjeman's poetry is enriched by a close acquaintance with the lines of poets who influenced him. Betjeman himself was quite open about the 'intertextual' nature of his poetic composition:

> First there is the thrilling or terrifying recollection of a place, a person or a mood which hammers inside the head saying 'Go on! Go on! It is your duty to make a poem out of it'. Then a line or a phrase suggests itself. Next comes the selection of a metre. I am a traditionalist in metres and have made few experiments. The rhythms of Tennyson, Crabbe, Hawker, Dowson, Hardy, James Elroy Flecker, Moore and Hymns A & M are generally buzzing about in my brain and I choose one from these which seems to me to suit the theme.[10]

However, a distinction needs to be made between (inevitable) poetic influence in the composition of a poem and poetry that relies, for important effects, on resonating certain literary allusions. Betjeman's poetry is surely of the first kind, whereas Eliot's earlier poetry is of the second – although the multiplicity of poetic 'parallels' cited in Christopher Ricks's Notes to the misnamed *Inventions of the March Hare*[11] does not persuade me that this should be carried beyond what is implicitly 'flagged'. The most important influence from Betjeman's loved precursors is, surely, the modelling of metrical and rhythmic modes of 'containment'. Here, for all their later friendship, Betjeman's 'American master' scarcely helped him. Eliot and Hopkins are, the poet wrote in a letter to Frederick Booker, 'though great poets . . . dead ends. Their influences on style, ear and syntax are deplorable' (*LI* 437). Here, atypically, the 'teddy bear to the nation' begins to sound like F. R. Leavis – though to opposite critical effect. The defence of one's chosen means of 'containment' is clearly a passionate matter.

However, 'containment' is not only a matter of oral formalities but also, very much, a function of narrative strategy. Robin

11

Robertson has aptly commented on this phenomenon by way of analogy: ' "To enclose is to make sacred" ... That is what art does. A photographer, for instance ... will isolate, crop and frame an image. For me, poetry is about making the commonplace miraculous, making the moment huge ... '.[12] In this, somewhat bizarrely, Betjeman's technique may be seen as incipiently 'postmodern' in the terms that Jean-François Lyotard has laid down – a mistrust of 'metanarrative' in favour of specific 'petits récits'. For instance, 'Death in Leamington' (called the poet's 'Lake Isle of Innisfree' by Bevis Hillier) is precisely such a 'récit' – the bedroom, the crochet, the nurse, the routine, the revelation, the gas-tap. Another way of describing such technique is Eliot's well-known 'objective correlative'. Indeed, while this has often been discussed in neo-*Symboliste* terms as a matter of figural collage (the 'logic of the imagination'), the concept was first devised to comment on the dramatic action in *Hamlet*:

> The only way of expressing emotion in the form of art is by finding an 'objective correlative'; in other words, a set of objects, a situation, a chain of events which shall be the formula of that *particular* emotion; such that when the external facts which must terminate in sensory experience, are given, the emotion is immediately evoked.[13]

This is brilliantly proposed; but Eliot then proceeds, far more controversially, to take exception to Shakespeare's plot: 'nothing that Shakespeare can do with the plot can express Hamlet for him', for the hero's emotion 'is in excess of the facts as they appear'. The 'objective correlative', then, is a matter of encasing feelings within a 'formula' of 'events'. In this regard, Betjeman's poetry strategy accords with Eliot's theory pretty exactly.

'The Arrest of Oscar Wilde at the Cadogan Hotel' is an early example of this. The 'situation' and 'set of objects' are largely provided by the hotel itself (index of Wilde's 'world') – hock and seltzer, lace, bell-rope, 'palms on the staircase'. This and the rather stagy dramatic dialogue ('Dear boy', 'come for tew take yew') create the 'chain of events' that authorize the emotion: 'He staggered – and, terrible-eyed ... ' (*CP* 17). The tension is created by contrast – 'Robbie' (Ross) to the 'PLAIN CLOTHES POLICEMAN', Oxford English to Cockney, *The Yellow Book* to courtroom indictment, the Cadogan to the looming Reading Gaol. Minimalist detailing is charged with 'atmosphere' so that 'the emotion is immediately evoked'. Granted the enduring power of the Wilde myth (and its constant redeployment in the ongoing politicization of sexuality and gender), this poem ranks as a significant 1930s 'intervention', and on a theme Betjeman will return to in, for instance, 'Monody on the Death of a Platonist Bank Clerk' (*CP* 273–4). However, the main point here is that 'containment' of feeling within the 'objective correlative' is a mode of narrative development. From the static lace curtains to the waiting hansom carriage, the poem outlines a fable of brain against brawn, class against class, sexual transgression against gender conventionality. And the art is very much in the detail. John Buchan, for instance (novelistic forerunner of James Bond machismo and a future Governor General of Canada), has infiltrated the pages of the literary organ of Aestheticism. 'The times they are a'changin'.'

It is worthwhile trying to tie down the kinds of 'petit récit' that characterize the Betjeman *œuvre*, since they help indicate the kinds of emotion the poems 'encase'. These concern, in particular, themes of death, love, religion, childhood, landscape, and the barbarism that attends change. The poems essentially express feelings ('I could not *think*'). And feelings, in Betjeman, are closely associated with the faculty of seeing acutely. Out of this amalgam the poet typically creates a narrative, with a structured beginning, middle, and end. In 'Exeter', for instance (*CP* 33–4), the doctor's wife is introduced as a lapsed Christian, but at the end ('Now...') the Cathedral bells call to her again, while the middle part of the poem relates the death of her husband, the catalyst for change. In 'Youth and Age on Beaulieu River, Hants' (*CP* 110–11), the old woman's lonely meditation is given structure by the setting-out of a girl's boat, the rowing expedition, and the eventual return. In 'Hertfordshire' (*CP* 225–6), the protagonist's complex feelings for his father are expressed through a kind of double narrative – an earlier visit to the county on a shooting expedition followed by a later visit (with extended description) after his father is dead. Many characteristic Betjeman poems are precisely 'balladic' because feeling is conveyed through recounting events – a nurse discovers a woman's dead body; a subaltern woos and wins an athletic girl; a woman is recalled to faith by her husband's sudden death; a visit with father, and one to the same place after his death; or (in 'The

Village Inn' (*CP* 192–4)) the poet outlines, by satiric contrast, the metamorphosis of the old pub into the 'sanit'ry' new one. All this does not mean that the poet's work is reduced to chronological realism – 'real' time and story time may be handled with novelistic subtlety. But the storytelling itself is of the essence in most cases. The story is what 'encase's the emotion.

Yet quite frequently the emotion is mainly contained by non-narrative means – for instance, by 'simultaneous' topographical description. Here the evocation of place rather than the development of a story is the predominant method. An obvious example is 'Henley-on-Thames' (*CP* 84). Although various activities are recorded in the poem, there is no story as such – just an evocation of place from a position of static observation: 'As here stand I.' The effect is rather that of a framed painting, in which the detailing slowly builds up a particularized vision of Englishness – river, houseboat, bridge, evening mist. I shall say more about 'place-myth' in the third chapter. Here it is the containing function of description that needs to be stressed. A neo-Joycean 'epiphany' is built up in terms of poignant particularities. As an anthropologist has recently written: 'landscape becomes the most generally accessible and widely shared *aide-memoire* of a culture's knowledge and understanding of its past and future.'[14] Betjeman's landscape poems typically frame a scene where a held present moment contains the past, but also intimates a future.

In 'Greenaway' (*CP* 184–5) the social dimension of landscape is largely missing (but for the stile, path, and washed-up coal): the scene becomes psychologized. This is effected by adding a dream scenario to the evocation of the 'small and smelly bay'. An element of fearful fantasy is conjured out of the strongly breaking seas. The poem can be seen as a 'container' for personal terror at possible helplessness and extinction, where Greenaway-as-place is merely a trigger scene. Another place might have served as well to summon up the awesome 'water-world'. Where Henley remains specific (the particular), Green-away becomes a kind of topographic 'Fear Death by Water' (the universal). Yet it may well be that the poet would have preferred the particular – as safer, for 'Greenaway' intimates the limits of 'containment' – its structural fragility in relation to the emotional engulfment it seeks to tame.

14

In practice, 'balladic' and topographic modes frequently come combined in Betjeman's poetry – and, of course, the poet deploys other literary modes too, such as satire, eulogy, and elegy. A familiar combination of the two main modes could be called 'topographical narrative'. In 'Sunday Afternoon Service in St Enodoc's Church, Cornwall' (CP 113–17), for instance, a discernible story is unfolded. The poem commences with a companionable 'Come on! come on!', as if the reader becomes part of the action. The 'tinny bell' draws 'all things' to worship, and a small collection of characters is described as on their way (across the golf course) to the church, while a couple resist the appeal. A personalized protagonist emerges about a third of the way into the poem, and it is his sensations and reflections, during the service, that then dominate the progression. Unlike Philip Larkin's 'Church Going', the persona is knowledgeable about church architecture and furnishings, and he is somewhat wry about the lassitude of the bell-ringer, organist, and clergyman. But then he appears to doze off himself as the poem moves into portentous topographic mode (somewhat borrowing from *King Lear* to describe the gull). We are in cliff and wave terrain again. The poem is written in blank verse – iambic pentameter provides a more elastic 'container' than the quatrain form. At times, though, the metre is used with somewhat wooden exactitude – 'Have better chance than I to last the storm.' Yet the breaking wave is rendered with neo-Wordsworthian sonority:

> Now she breaks
> And in an arch of thunder plunges down
> To burst and tumble, foam on top of foam,
> Criss-crossing, baffled, sucked and shot again,
> A waterfall of whiteness...

The fearsome seascape seems to conjure back the saint who chose it for his meditation, resulting in the building of the church. He dwelt with God, who presided over the lives and (often tragic) deaths of local sailors, lying now in the graveyard. But then the church harmonium brings us back to the immediate service and Psalm 14 is announced: presumably the rest of the service is yet to come. The narrative subsumes action and reflection into devotion.

Blank verse, as 'container', is the main vehicle of Betjeman's autobiographical sequence *Summoned by Bells* (1960). In a prefatory note, the poet somewhat bizarrely defends his decision not to write 'in prose'. 'He chose blank verse, because he found it best suited to brevity and the rapid change of mood and subject.' Prose can, surely, 'suit' brevity (Samuel Beckett) or 'rapid changes of mood' (Virginia Woolf). Perhaps Betjeman is really defending the comparative looseness of form in *Summoned* in relation to the 'rhythm and rhyme' of his best-known poems. It is likely, in fact, that he had Wordsworth's *The Prelude* in mind as model – a classic of variable Romantic blank verse – although the project is less to trace the 'Growth of a Poet's Mind' than to outline the development of his sensibility. Compared to Wordsworth's poem (or the prose *recherches* of Proust or Dorothy Richardson), Betjeman's project is modest, cropped down, and idiosyncratically stylish. Its fey excesses ('O Peggy Purey-Cust, how pure you were') or banalities ('Can it really be/That this same carriage came from Waterloo?') are scarcely the fault of the metre chosen. Blank verse does well enough as 'reflecting' voice – although it may be helpful to many of us to suppress recollections of the poet's own reading voice, and hear it more as if intoned by Jeremy Irons in the televised *Brideshead Revisited*: 'Balkan Sobranies in a wooden box,/The college arms upon the lid; Tokay...'(*SBB* 93).

Betjeman worked at his 'epic' over a considerable number of years. The resultant poem came after much writing and rewriting. And, while the poet appears to have relied considerably on line-by-line advice from such as Tom Driberg, the most important choice for literary 'encase'-ment seems to have been his alone – the division into nine discrete 'chapters'. If we exclude the somewhat tacked-on addition, 'The Cricket Master', the overall movement of the poem is more like *Paradise Lost* than *The Prelude*. After a privileged middle-class upbringing and private-sector education, our hero revels in the social life of gay Oxford – and is finally sent down for failing a Divinity exam. Following this, the world lies all before him in the almost mythical invocation of Gabbitas Thring. 'Start of a poet', as Glyn Maxwell has recently written of himself.[15] The 'tragic' action confirms the protagonist's long-felt destiny for art – with a salute to his 'earlier publisher and friend' (*SBB* 111). This is, as it were, *Jude the Obscure* turned upside down: not the exclusion of a scholar but the expulsion of an aesthete. Yet where Hardy's novel is imbued with bitterness, Betjeman's poem is commendably equable: tutorials, dons, and academic assessment were 'neither here nor there' for the poet or his friends. Resorting to poetic formality, the poet seals up this part of his own story. There is a gutsiness and inner serenity behind the 'Personality' of the guffawing old codger.

The chapters of the poem develop progressively. I–IX constitute a symmetrical poetic schema – three times three: an exercise in 'triune' meditation about the one life. 'Before MCMXIV' is a classic of Edwardian Age mythologization, and ends suitably with Archibald, the teddy bear. 'The Dawn of Guilt' replays a modern motif of Fathers and Sons, and intimates a poetic vocation. 'Highgate' outlines early school experience and ends with an enigmatic response from a poetic father figure, 'Mr. Eliot'. 'Cornwall in Childhood' captures the magic of youthful seaside holidays, and draws a line around them ('Safe'). 'Private School' is a 'prep'-narrative, indicating a growing love of architecture and ending with a provisional 'lyrical ballad'. 'London' updates, as it were, Book IV of Wordsworth's *Prelude* – but adds to trams and tube-trains a growing love of church worship. 'Marlborough', although acutely personalized, replays a *Tom Brown's Schooldays* theme, as many books have done: it ends with the gift of a friend's photograph. 'Cornwall in Adolescence' memorializes growing family tensions, open defiance of father, and an exploration of growing freedom. 'The Opening World' is all Oxford memoirs – new friendships, high jinks, and endless partying. Overall, then, *Summoned by Bells* represents a verse *Bildungsroman*, indeed a *Künstleroman*. And, as evidenced above, the poem draws on a number of novelistic sub-genres. Generic form, then, also 'encase's in its way. It is a means of making sense of the poet's memories, of creating a poem out of what has been lived. The nine sections effect an aesthetic shaping – a means of controlling, making consolatory and rendering experience shareable.

The urge to share was fundamental to Betjeman, as poet, essayist, broadcaster, and wit. He was, above all, a communicator; to get things across was more important to him than to 'MAKE IT NEW'. This helps explain his reliance on traditional forms

17

and his kinship with poets who remain popular. John Press has noticed his similarity to Kipling (patriotism, sensitiveness, loneliness), John Sparrow put him in the tradition of Crabbe and Cowper, and all critics acknowledge his closeness to Tennyson, while the poet himself stressed his love of Hardy. He was, as Bevis Hillier suggests, 'taken by the idea of a special language reserved for poetry'; the most popular poets had established such a language, and their precedent makes it likely that (as William Plomer has commented): 'his use of iambics suggests that he finds them not only traditional but idiomatically natural for the utterance of an English poet'[16] – not necessarily in pentameter, however. Yet, if the bottles are old, the wine is new in many ways: Hillier argues that 'with all his Tennysonian chimes, he has more in common with Eliot and Auden'.[17] In important senses that is true – and both Auden and Eliot admired Betjeman's work. But, by contrast, he is unadventurous, and his *œuvre* scarcely develops – as theirs does. The themes and moods of his last poems are much like those in his first – and the aesthetic mode of 'containment' remains constant.

For this reason there is no *annus mirabilis* or 'golden decade' of Betjeman's verse. John Press states that *First and Last Loves* is 'his most substantial book', while Patrick Taylor-Martin avers that 'Betjeman's finest achievement remains the poems of *A Few Late Chrysanthemums*'.[18] Both judgements leave far too many memorable poems out of the reckoning and so are scarcely viable. Even Bevis Hillier's (edited) *Uncollected Poems* include verses one would not wish to be without. In any case, the 'common reader' (and Betjeman has had a larger than normal share of these) is likely to pick favourites from earliest work to latest, without need of critical pronunciations. And that choice would depend on what aspects of the poet's work are most valued – suburban satire, seascapes, religious striving, historical ballad, rural topography, childhood poems, verse autobiography, and so forth. Probably the most contentious critical question is how one compares *Summoned by Bells* to the rest of the Betjeman canon. It tends to get pride of place on local library tapes of the poet reading: but this partly indicates the success of Betjeman as 'television personality' (he was a consummate media-marketer of his individual brand of charm), and the sequence remains difficult to assess in the same terms as, say, 'Hymn' or 'Love in a Valley' or 'Henley-on-Thames'. As will become evident in the next chapter, I find *Summoned* interesting for what it represents concerning 'masculinity' and Englishness; however, some of the verse seems rather second rate compared to the poet's finest achievements.

'St. Saviour's, Aberdeen Park, Highbury, London, N.' (*CP* 126–7) is an example of such fine achievement – chosen here partly to offset the main emphasis on the quatrain. The poem consists of six verses of six lines each, rhymed ABABAB in each verse. The rhythm is trickier than in many of Betjeman's poems, and overall flow is only established after some idiosyncratic 'oral' try-outs: 'With oh such peculiar branching'; 'Stop the trolley-bus, stop!' or:

> And here, where the roads unite
> Of weariest worn-out London – no cigarettes, no beer,
> No repairs undertaken, nothing in stock – alight...

The surprise negation of cigarettes and beer seems to signal a kicking-away of habitual props – an 'unaccommodated' facing of home truths. The psychic resonance of this has already been set up in the first verse: 'that ever-increasing spire/Bulges over the housetops' – a veritable tripwire for psychoanalytic speculation. Yet such implications are held within a brilliantly exact evocation of period-social detail: trolley-bus, tradesman's entrance, Italianate houses – which hedge about the central symbolization, the 'great Victorian church'. The church is intimately significant to parental courtship and marriage, rather as in Michèle Roberts's lovely poem 'The Return' ('I believe in the big ribbed boat/...the man and woman build/ with the sweat of love').[19] The architectural detailing Betjeman adored is overwhelmed by the force of emotion:

> Great red church of my parents, cruciform crossing they knew –
>
> .   .   .   .
>
> Bound through a red-brick transept for a once familiar pew...

The protagonist kneels in the chancel. He thinks of the Eucharistic 'Bread'; a Freudian might see this as 'female' ('so white and small'); a Christian would see it simply as sacramental. And this sets up the ending – 'primal scene' subsumed into what makes any such thing possible:

the Power which sends the shadows up this polychrome wall,
  Is God who created the present, the chain-smoking millions and me;
Beyond the throb of the engines is the throbbing heart of all –
  Christ, at this Highbury altar, I offer myself to Thee.

'Wall' – 'all', 'me '– 'Thee' – this is to 'encase'. And while the containing power of rhyme (and rhythm) harks back to the primal psyche, it also serves to anchor, in poetic formality, a profoundly unsettling meditation on spiritual belief, social appearances, and ideological myths. As we shall see, Betjeman's poetry does not so much conform to convention as profoundly unsettle normal assumptions about masculinity, Englishness, and Christianity. To adapt Umberto Eco's neat phrase about Thomas Aquinas's canonization, the 'Fire Chief' of middle-class convention was, in fact, the 'big arsonist'.[20] In effecting this, Betjeman used the armature of traditional form – a 'crustacean' self-protective strategy ('The fan-shaped scallop shells, the backs of crabs' (*SBB* 34)). The poet's ruse is to clothe personal fear, weakness, anger, rapture, or reverence in traditional dress. It is an ultimately 'camp' strategy – the neo-Parnassian quatrain, for instance, as play area, pantomime space, or carnivalesque market square. Out of neo-Victorian verse-forms he creates something between the documentary and the Surreal.

In a thought-provoking book, *Poetry and Phantasy*, Antony Easthope has proposed the formula: 'Poetry as Social Phantasy'. He writes: *'the literary text always produces ideological and phantasy meanings in a simultaneity. '* He further elaborates:

> a single poem cannot be considered apart from its intertextual relation to other texts in an ideological formation... Within textual discourse itself, aesthetic discourse constitutes a specific mode; the requirements of poetic discourse exemplified in the material operation of the signifier in poetry through metre and verse form make a further degree of particularity.[21]

Betjeman's 'metre and verse form' eschew modernist experimentation and become bedded within the carapace of the populist poetry of his boyhood – this constitutes that 'intertextual relation to other texts' that John Sparrow has referred to in more belletristic terms.

The success of the poet's strategy is evidenced in his wide

reader following. Yet the appeal to such readers is attained less by 'natural' suburban balladry than by subtle poetic redeployments – the poet was, after all, an advertising expert who coined slogans for Shell Oil. A 'shell' is a neat 'container', which he used to combine motoring romance and an English never-never land.[22] In the poetry, Englishness is no more commercialized than in, say, Ford Madox Ford's *Parade's End* or Derek Jarman's *The Last of England*. Yet it is constructed by techniques part learnt in advertising. The neo-Tennysonian formality is a 'cunning disguise'. It is postmodernly self-conscious – and, at times, close to self-parody:

> Tonight we feel the muffled peal
> Hang on the village like a pall....

('Uffington' (*CP* 264))

Betjeman loved bells, and parish churches, and especially that of Uffington (where he was a Church Warden). The poem brings such things to memorable realization; yet it is euphoniously self-mocking too, perhaps:

> Imprisoned in a cage of sound
> Even the trivial seems profound.

2

A Man, My Son

'Well now, my boy, I want your solemn word
To carry on the firm when I am gone:
Fourth generation, John – they'll look to you.'

(SBB 16)

Betjeman's 'Dawn of Guilt' has everything to do with fathers
and sons, as with sons and 'lovers', and the labelling 'fourth
generation' is repeated in *Summoned by Bells*. Paternal law
becomes reinforced by maternal blackmail: ' "He *is* your father,
John!" ' (*SBB* 85) – and elsewhere: ' "When I am dead you will be
sorry, John" ' (*SBB* 60). Early on in this autobiographical poem,
an issue is made of the patriarchal name – German or Dutch?
One 'n' or two at the end? Where now political correctness
might prefer the name 'Betjeperson' to Betjemann (the father's
spelling) or Betjeman (the poet's), nationalist correctness, at that
time, concerned possible Germanicity – ' "Betjeman's a German
spy –" ' (*SBB* 28). This now appears rather *Riddle of the Sands*
stuff, yet it is arguably similar to Sylvia Plath's conflictual
ambivalence about her name, her father, and her Germanic
inheritance ('Ich, ich, ich, ich').[1] Critics have followed the poet's
lead in highlighting this odd importance of the poet's surname
(apparently the derivation *was* German), but less remarked is the
way the Christian name 'John' is almost invariably deployed in
the poem as a reinforcement of exhortation, accusation, reproval,
or condescension. It punctuates the text like a bell-toll of
imputed blame. Perhaps the main transition in the 'Cricket
Master' addendum is that suddenly 'John' is replaced by 'Sir'.
However disillusioning his later prospects, at least the 'artist' is
not quite now a 'young man'.

General public perceptions about poetry have peculiarly

interesting relevance to the theme of masculinity – which I take to be a core motif in *Summoned by Bells*. For instance, in 1995 a British television poll connected with 'Poetry Week' found that the nation's favourite poems were: (1) Rudyard Kipling's 'If'; (2) Alfred Lord Tennyson's 'The Lady of Shalott'; (3) Walter de la Mare's 'The Listeners'. In more recent polls such poems have remained highly popular. The 1995 national 'Number 1' poem constitutes, in fact, a versified do-it-yourself construction kit for mainstream male Englishness. It can be summed up as, 'Keep your head – and be a real man'. The second choice is focused on the familiar male anxiety as to 'what the woman wants'. Tennyson's answer appears to be: not the web and not the loom, but the Mr Knightley of the Matter of Britain, Sir Lancelot. And the third choice features an updated, horse-riding 'traveller' who keeps an appointment with some ghostly 'other' – ' "Tell them .../That I kept my word," he said'. In each case, an almost caricatural masculinity haunts the poem – and hence the poetry-reading public. *Summoned by Bells*, as Betjeman's *œuvre* overall, is provocative (for all its middle-class cosiness) precisely because it unsettles conventional ideas about what 'being a man' is all about. But then, arguably, the choice of a poetic vocation is, itself, a 'feminine' move in the traditional English gender game.

The issue of male identity and motivation has received a great deal of academic attention in the late 1990s. Most studies have paid, at least, lip-service to the ideas of Sigmund Freud, who, self-confessedly baffled by women's deepest desires, used the figure of the 'artist' to spell out what he saw as the bottom line of masculine aspiration: 'honour, power and the love of women'.[2] Much earlier in history, Saint Augustine (a 'patriarch' if ever, though one Betjeman might have agreed with) formulated a very different answer, generalizing desire as universal: 'Man is one of your creatures, Lord, and his instinct is to praise you ... The thought of you stirs him so deeply that he cannot be content unless he praises you, because you have made us for yourself and our hearts find no peace until they rest in you.'[3] By contrast, the Marxist slogan 'from each according to his [*sic*] abilities to each according to his needs' hypostasizes materialistic men (and 'material girls') who are content to live by bread alone. And yet, from materially bountiful America, Robert Bly has lamented the emergence of a 'soft' male and evoked a compensatory 'warrior power' that 'nourished on electronic or magnetic energy, moves behind the veil of flesh, and alters moods and impulses, shines through the skin and bones, makes the body do what the power wants'.[4] Clearly masculine motivation has become a major teaser: the wonder is that it has taken so long for it to be recognized as such. In *Summoned by Bells*, Betjeman acknowledges, constantly, a male norm, yet portrays himself as different from it ('what was my own?' (*SBB* 107)). Archibald the teddy bear, established on the second page, becomes the symbol of a sly, but determined, otherness.

In a helpful 'introductory text', *Understanding Masculinities* (1996),[5] emphasis is laid less on the system of 'Patriarchy' than on issues that Betjeman, himself, addresses – family (and hence psychic) dynamics, schooling, work role (or lack of it), a sense of 'others' (for the adult, heterosexual male – women, boys, homosexuals, etc.), and the importance of self-descriptive stories. Betjeman stresses the first of these particularly. Family dynamics underlie and help form the budding poet. The issue is brought to a head in Chapter VIII, 'Cornwall in Adolescence'. The crucial confrontation is set up ('encase'd) by a double narrative: first the evocation of father's impatient car drive down to Cornwall (epic purposefulness); then the description of mother's sedentary meditations ('feminine' waiting):

> Two more hours of quiet bliss!
> From this verandah I can see the world
> And be at one with Nature. Think Good Thoughts,
> And merge myself into the Infinite.
> There's Ethel Harden coming up the lane...

(*SBB* 82)

There is a quasi-Joycean irony in the way femininity is rendered through dramatized 'interior' language, suffused by the idiom of light reading: 'As rang the martyred wife's or mother's cry/In many a Temple Thurston she had read' (*SBB* 85). As the anti-heroic narrator says, he loved his mother more, but so became more critical of her artlessness. Father is *feared*.

The crisis occurs at breakfast – the father's wrath directed first at his wife and the maid, then at the late-rising protagonist. Masculinity is physicalized: 'Bang! Boom! His big fists set the cups a-dance' (*SBB* 84). A paternal programme is wrathfully announced: ' "I'll keep you at it as I've kept myself – " ' (*SBB* 84). At this point Archie's 'idolator' asserts an unwonted 'normal' masculinity of his own: ' "You damn well won't!" ' (*SBB* 84). He summons up his own physicality – 'slammed the door against my father's weight' (*SBB* 85). The protagonist runs off shouting ' "I'm free!" ' But, as in such ur-texts as *A Portrait of the Artist* or *Sons and Lovers*, the question remains: free for what? It takes the rest of the poem to tease out some of the possibilities, which are never really resolved. After Oxford, the 'allowance' – temporary middle-class investment in the filial *rites-de-passage* – is cut off. A fraternal voice later confirms the closure of the arrangement: ' "Your father's right, John; you must earn your keep" ' (*SBB* 110). Becoming a cricket master is not, of course, what the poet sees as any long-term solution. Beyond the 'containment' of the poem, Betjeman would eventually pioneer a life through the world of oil money, journalism, advertising, book publication, and television appearances. This 'signifying absence' is scarcely hinted at until the very end: 'Richer, wickeder and colder,/ Fuller too of care, Cat Hill' (*SBB* 115). In real life, the poet's self-announced male rebellion would culminate in terms both father and mother must have approved – popular writer, loved 'Personality', Poet Laureate, and Knight of the Realm. There is none of this in the poem. *Summoned by Bells* constitutes a narrative of masculine self-exploration in how not to be what your parents want – a text of guilt and partial reparation, yet also of affirmation for 'the road less travelled by'.

Schooling is, also, a major theme – arguably *the* major theme in so far as masculinity constitutes an ultimately social phenomenon. Betjeman's represented experience has minority particularity (the 'private'-education sector) but major significance in terms of the acculturation of the traditional English ruling class. It reads as an education of increasing privilege, whatever the protagonist's aversion to aspects of it – a development the poet points up rather than suppresses partly due to his cheery tendency to name-drop. Nurse Sarah's efforts (formative for a fear of Hell and physical beatings) lead on to an introduction to father's Firm and a growing acquaintance with North London and middle-class holidays. Byron House brings first love in the form of fated Peggy, but also the world of schoolboy bullying (our anti-hero inevitable victim rather than perpetrator). Highgate Junior School days

correspond with the outbreak of the First World War –
Kitchener's poster slogan conjoined in boyish mythology with
Tiger Tim and Bonnie Bluebell: compared to Wordsworth's
'shades of the prison-house', this 'growing boy' develops into a
late modern (proleptically postmodern) opening hyperworld of
mass journalism, advertising, and government propaganda.
(Betjeman would later prove adept in each of these fields – the
last in Ireland during the Second World War). There occurs
another bullying experience but then a discovery of poetry –
'Hemans, Campbell, Longfellow and Scott/...Edgar Allan Poe'
(*SBB* 29). The protagonist begins writing poems himself, and it is
typical of the poet's 'luck' that a Mr Eliot should be on hand to
receive *The Best of Betjeman*. If 'too kind to say' what he thought of
this juvenilia, biographies suggest that the 'Pope of Russell
Square' would have been happy to publish later Betjeman, if
given the chance.

The protagonist's world unfolds further in terms of 'Scott's
Emulsion', Euthymol, hygiene, and electricity (*SBB* 33).
Betjeman's acute social sense would always be grounded, as
here, in finely registered metonymic particularities of the
contemporary, whatever his sponsorship of historic parish
churches and country houses. An extended holiday sequence
in Cornwall widens the poet's 'photographic' depiction of
contemporary middle-class life, and introduces a 'Girl Guide-y'
virago, Miss Usher, who offers a typically snobbish verdict on
the young protagonist. The chapter 'Private School' then
constructs a modern (archetypal) 'prep.'-land, where English
maleness has been played out, in this century, 'against the Hun'.
The opening description is wonderfully parodic of English
masculine stereotyping (including Virginia Woolf's idealized
Percival in *The Waves*):

> Percival Mandeville, the perfect boy,
> Was all a schoolmaster could wish to see –
> Upright and honourable, good at games,
> Well-built, blue-eyed; a sense of leadership
> Lifted him head and shoulders from the crowd...
>
> (*SBB* 43)

The sheer funniness of the apparently deadpan description
helps indicate how subversive Betjeman's 'take' on young

26

manhood can be. Quite why this cardboard young gent should want to fight poetic John is not clear (surely he was not that 'unsporting, mean or base'); but then the anecdote is clearly set up to emphasize the protagonist's cunning stratagem – '"mater's very ill"' (*SBB* 44). The strong Mandevillean arm of comfort (no doubt gratifying in its own way) is of far less importance than the demonstration of evolving Betjemanian guile. Where Joyce chose silence, exile, and cunning, Betjeman chooses rhetorical invention, chumminess, and deception.

The First World War intrudes again into the narrative at this point. Betjeman walks a tightrope over the reality, balancing elegy with schoolboy defensive humour. He shows how formed and forming masculinities react differently to news from the Front:

> Sometimes his gruff old voice was full of tears...
>
> (*SBB* 44)

> the trenches and the guns
> Meant less to us than bicycles and gangs...
>
> (*SBB* 45)

However, 'gangs' provide the bonding out of which platoons and regiments are formed: in the twentieth century, total war, and compulsory enlistment, have been the male inheritance. Betjeman's physique later prevented him from having a combat role in the armed services. During the Second World War he became, instead, a cultural attaché in Dublin, seeking to persuade the grudge-laden Irish that the average Percival Mandeville was somewhat preferable to Adolf Hitler: the IRA (with its usual political delicacy) planned to assassinate teddy bear John – but failed. World war was, in fact, the dark horizon against which the poet's quirky Englishness played itself out. Betjeman's engaging bonhomie is exercised in an acknowledged wasteland: 'The latest names of those who'd lost their lives' (*SBB* 44).

Father figures are shown playing an important role in the making of the protagonist's ambivalent masculinity. In Chapter V, Gerald Haynes is the first of these: 'Much do I owe this formidable man/...his kindness and his power to share' (*SBB* 48–9). Haynes is shown as fostering the protagonist's love of nature and church architecture. In Chapter VII, Mr Hughes takes over to add a 'skill' factor – the art of sketching. In VIII, the priest of St Ervan's church plays a similar role, lending a copy of Arthur Machen's *Secret Glory*. In IX, Kolkhorst, Bowra, and Rowse provide a quasi-paternalism ('Alma Pater') to broaden the poet's sense of manhood's possibilities, and so make it seem impossible to return to Betjeman père's world of 'samples, invoices and stock' (*SBB* 110). By then, of course, many of the poet's peers were – well – Peers.

Wordsworth has written about being 'fostered alike by beauty and by fear'. With suburban modifications, the phrase fits Betjeman's narrative too. The 'encase'ment of beauty is the goal – but the described reality may be fear: the sense of 'an impending doom' (*SBB* 66). The Marlborough experience remained to haunt the poet ('Be fair!'). Yet, for all the miseries of 'early school', constipation, and the melodramatic 'basket', schooling at Marlborough exonerates the protagonist from being a 'rotter' ('"The boys know best"' (*SBB* 70)), and it provides him with further opportunities to explore the world and himself. With reference to the latter, 'desire' has become a factor. As with Peggy Purey-Cust, and later Biddy Walsham, there is a powerful idealization in early erotic experience, as rendered:

> He sat among the harebells in his shorts,
> Hugging his knees till I caught up with him.
> A lock of hair kept falling on his face...

> (*SBB* 73)

As the poet puts it: 'Here was love' – but declaration or touch were, at the time, out of bounds. Beauty, in the flesh, becomes an important Betjemanian theme. And there is a gilded homo/hetero ambivalence in the way Betjeman works out the *mythos* of love. In fact, there's a touch of 'Derek Jarman' within the poet's post-pre-Raphish cult of the body beautiful. And overall is a 'camp' incarnationalism, an ultimately Neoplatonic aesthetic religiosity.

Oxford is represented as the perfect culmination of the protagonist's dreams. It plays on place-myth advertisement as shamelessly as Larkin in 'Dockery and Son' – or an 'Inspector Morse' trailer:

My wide-sashed windows looked across the grass
To tower and hall and lines of pinnacles.
The wind among the elms, the echoing stairs,
The quarters, chimed across the quiet quad...

(*SBB* 93)

The 'education' the protagonist acquires seems almost entirely
to do with personal reading and, above all, the conversation
with friends – Harold Acton, Osbert Lancaster, Major Attlee (at
Sezincote lunches), Harman Grisewood, Emlyn Williams, W. H.
Auden and Tom Driberg, to name-drop a few. Betjeman's
Oxford reads not as a seat of learning but as an upper-class
social club: and he expects readers to be interested in it as such.
(They are – as for thinking, our *savants* will do that for us.) What
matters is social tone – for example, Harry Strathspey coming to
a champagne party after dining at Blenheim (*SBB* 94). Needless
to say, William Shakespeare, William Blake, John Keats, Basil
Bunting, or Simon Armitage would not qualify to join in such
jolly junketings. Yet such is the middle-class mythology of the
Oxbridge poet that this university experience is made to appear
a 'natural' birthright. English poetry is supposed to spring
effortlessly from acquaintance with the Isis or Cam – poetry
publishing too (by one's 'chums') – and poets should normally
have knowledge of such 'rhymes that rocked the room' as

G'uggery, G'uggery Nunc,
Your room is all cluttered with junk..

(*SBB* 97)

As Betjeman says, 'trivial and silly '– also wholly out of touch
with the 'felt experience' of England as a whole.

Summoned by Bells replicates (and celebrates) the traditional
Oxbridge distinction between rival modes of masculinity –
aesthetes and athletes, hearties and arties. ('Undergraduettes'
are out of it, their bicycles weighed down with books on Middle
English.) And out of this hothouse will come 'Administrators,
professorial chairs' (*SBB* 102), the due reward of a ' "very able
man" ', whether wrangler or rower. In our anti-hero's case (he
had wanted to become a 'don'), the requisite talent is not in
evidence. And his subsequent role as cricket master (presumably secured on the Magdalen connection) is doubly bogus: he
cannot play cricket, and he is expected to teach Divinity (a

subject he has just failed). Like Evelyn Waugh in *Decline and Fall*, the poem says as much about the idiocy of the old-boy syndrome as about the fecklessness of the protagonist's negotiation of his masculine role. Betjeman, however, does contrive to develop an individuality beyond the polarization of ' "raw meat with lilies" ' (*SBB* 94) and 'Bullingdonian brawl' (*SBB* 106). Eventually, it became highly marketable in terms of affable charm:

> There on the wooden bench outside The Cock
> Sat Barnstaple, Miss Spencer-Clarke and I,
> At last forgetful of tomorrow's dread
> And gazing into sky-blue Hertfordshire.

> (*SBB* 114)

If the issue of a career (or 'work role') is suspended in *Summoned by Bells*, a sense of the 'other', in the form of femininity, is not. Mother, nurse, maids, girls, aunts, girlfriends, mother figures, and so on offset Betjeman's *entrée* into English manhood. At times, representatives of the 'feminine' act as consolatory advisers. At an early point in the onset of puberty, his adopted Aunt Elsie is such a tutelary presence – waiting 'while we choked with rage' (*SBB* 89). Our protagonist wants to borrow 'the car' to take out Biddy Walsham, the girl he currently 'worships', and fantasizes that some sexual contact might occur, on 'the electron principle' (*SBB* 90). Aunt Elsie explains that he is still a boy – the word 'still' a crucial pivot – hence ' "it's sensible to walk" ' (*SBB* 90). The text seems to endorse her caution. Later, at Sezincote, Mrs Dugdale ('mother of us all' (*SBB* 99)) seems to perform a similar role for the young student: 'Sweet confidante in every tale of woe!' (*SBB* 100). At this 'second home', the love of the Colonel and his wife provides, also, a temporary 'containment'. The specifics of what passes between budding poet and surrogate mother are textually suppressed. But what matters, as is the way in such encounters, is the sharing, the trust, the emotional ambience:

> ...Mrs Dugdale snipped exotic shrubs
> With secateurs as on and on I talked.

> (*SBB* 100)

An orthodox psychoanalyst might find something threatening in those secateurs – but snipping shrubs may be snipping shrubs, and Mrs Dugdale sounds more like Virginia Woolf's Mrs Ramsay in *To The Lighthouse* than any castrating harridan. The importance of the encounter – as in actual psychoanalytic *practice*[6] – is the talking itself…on, and on, and on. In the talking is the 'cure' .

Betjeman's poetry, in general, is fertile ground for a psycho-analytic 'hermeneutics of suspicion'. On the one hand, Mrs Dugdale's 'trailing…dress' (*SBB* 99), on the other, strong female hands and tennis rackets enclosed in presses ('The Olympic Girl', (*CP* 186)). It all sounds, in such terms, weirdly fetishistic. However, towards the double millennium it may well be less Betjeman's advertised idiosyncrasies than Freud's hubristic 'theoretical' metanarratives that are in need of 'unpacking'. (And a girl's fantasized hand is scarcely more fetishistic than Freud's beloved cigars.) In *Summoned by Bells*, and elsewhere, Betjeman represents the way in which erotic desire may be diffused into physical particularities: that is a poet's job in an age of heightened sexual awareness, and there is no reason to pathologize it. Throughout, Betjeman's autobio-graphical poem mediates between homoerotic longings and heterosexual desire (for older women as for younger girls). What may be more important for the poet's overall vision, however, is the way *eros* can become transfigured into *agape*:

> And behind their frail partitions
> Business women lie and soak,
>
> .   .   .   .
>
> Rest you there, poor unbelov'd ones,
> Lap your loneliness in heat.
>
> ('Business Girls', (*CP* 181))

The whole project of *Summoned by Bells* is to utilize a 'self-descriptive' story to try and make sense of one young male life. The importance of 'Personalism' and the 'significance of narrative for personal identity' has been aptly addressed, at length, in a trilogy of books by Patrick Grant.[7] Among many other things, these books demonstrate and underline how personal narrative has a specific literary history in the 'Latin West' – one far older than, say, the 'subject' of liberal humanism. In Homer, Grant points out, there is almost no sense of the modern person. If arguably there is in the Psalms, Grant's main emphasis is on how

31

theological arguments about the persons within the Trinity lead on to Augustine's *Confessions* and the increasing evolution of personal self-consciousness. The *Confessions* constitutes a proto-type for both Wordsworth's *The Prelude* and *Summoned by Bells*. And beyond such come more contemporaneous instances such as Sylvia Plath's *Ariel*, Erica Jong's *Fear of Flying*, Derek Jarman's *Modern Nature*, or Ted Hughes's *Birthday Letters*. Arguably, 'confessional' television shows (Oprah Winfrey, for instance) are the postmodern extension of this literary development.

Betjeman's personal narrative is set up in terms of the traditional Western 'gaze': the poem starts 'Here...I see' (*SBB* 3). If sound provides 'encase'ment (summoned by *bells*), this constitutes containment for a highly visual imagination. Constable and Keats (lines 11 and 12) come together. In addition, the poem is written well after the experiences described, by one of the 'gramophonic, cinematic...Oxford set'.[8] Early on in the poem cinematic 'tracking' is used to evoke a particularized North London:

> 31 West Hill!
> At that hill's foot did London then begin,
> With yellow horse-trams clopping past the planes
> To grey-brick nonconformist Chetwynd Road
> And on to Kentish Town and barking dogs
> And costers' carts and crowded grocers' shops
> And Daniels' store, the local Selfridge's...
>
> (*SBB* 5)

The visuality is highly specific, socially aware, and acutely sensitive to brand names ('Bon Marché' and 'Electric Palace' in the next line). 'Personalism' is established within a moving scene where eye helps define an 'I'. And that 'I' is also subconsciously underpinned by a long tradition of the masculinist eye. What Betjeman effects is to update and soften the scenario with small, ordinary detailing.

Summoned by Bells is about the emergence of a quirkily distinctive masculinity: it is essentially a narrative of boyhood, constructed to trace the development of poet, architectural and social commentator, and television 'Personality'. Its chosen 'spots of time' seem calculated to underline the protagonist's sensitivity, curiosity, and appetite for life. The most telling moments are outside the framework of formal education, for an ironic sub-theme is the repressive nature of conventional upper-middle-class schooling, only relieved by the personalities of certain teachers (who might have been more at home in A. S. Neill's Summerhill). The Cornwall passages, for instance, indicate the alert individuality of the Betjeman the poet wanted to display:

> Childhood is measured out by sounds and smells
> And sights, before the dark of reason grows.
> Ears! Hear again the wild sou'westers whine!
> Three days on end would the September gale
> Slam at our bungalows; three days on end
> Rattling cheap doors and making tempers short.
> It mattered not, for then enormous waves
> House-high rolled thunderous on Greenaway,
> Flinging up spume and shingle to the cliffs.
> Unmoved amid the foam, the cormorant
> Watched from its peak...
>
> (SBB 38)

The cormorant, one feels, is a bit like John Betjeman the topographic *raconteur*. Budding poetic sensibility is somewhat coerced: 'Ears! Hear again...'. Yet the rhetorical device serves to nudge out and make prominent remembered details of *temps perdu*: the three-day timespan, the shaking doors and short tempers, the waves 'House-high' (a child's view – but literally true in Cornwall). The combination of spume and shingle also describes an experienced reality – witness the average seaside promenade after a storm. Yet the real poetic work is in the sound, the rhythm: 'House-high rolled thunderous on Greenaway'; that very much captures the way a huge wave breaks ('thunderous') and hisses back – green away indeed!

The London passages too powerfully evoke a childhood world of vivid impressions, and of male adventure: Ronald Wright and the poet exploring the London Underground 'all day' (SBB 56). The evocation of a companion is important here, for Betjeman's represented boyhood becomes very much a development out of introspective sensitivity into appreciative gregariousness. The poet widens his horizons with a little help from his friends. So 'Metroland' is shared, and the social sphere is explored in implicit dialogism: 'We knew the different railways by their smells' (SBB 57). And growing awareness, in this passage, is very much a tale of male relationship in negotiating incipient masculine adulthood: 'we would talk/Loud gibberish in angry argument,/Pretending to be foreign' (*SBB* 57). The use of game-playing, jokiness, and verbal display has traditionally constituted a peculiarly male *rite de passage* (the television programme 'Have I Got News For You' would be a contemporary equivalent).

Yet the poet is careful to maintain a sense of personal solitude well into adolescence. In Chapter VIII, for instance, the unitary, Western male self is insisted upon as a credential for integrity: 'An only child, deliciously apart...' (*SBB* 88). There is, of course, a retrospective irony in this adolescent self-presentation – somewhere between young Werther and Adrian Mole. Yet, however absurd, such narcissistic self-posturing remains highly marketable – from Hamlet and Lord Byron to James Dean, Jimi Hendrix, Freddy Mercury, or Kurt Cobain. Luckily, our anti-hero has an aunt who takes him at his own 'reckoning' (*SBB* 89), but is also able to help him be 'sensible' (*SBB* 90).

In Chapter IX, 'The Opening World', our protagonist's incipient gregariousness is, indeed, opened out. The student Betjeman is less J. Alfred Prufrock than a 'wannabe' young Falstaff: 'Within those rooms I met my friends for life' (*SBB* 102). Friendship would become of key importance in the poet's lexicon of values; it remains, surely, a virtue – even if social envy might wish to carp at the upper-class nature of the friends Betjeman cultivated. And, if we take seriously the poet's darker, lonely side (surely we must), then the fact of a generous chumminess helps grant the poems the sane balance that characterizes them. The ageing Betjeman put this simply:

> I made hay while the sun shone.
> My work sold.
>
> .   .   .   .   .   .
>
> Give me the bonus of laughter
> As I lose hold.

> ('The Last Laugh', *CP* 341)

Laughter was the poet's mode of *entrée* into the 'Georgoisie', the secret of his populist 'Personality' and his refuge against despair. It is a highly social mode of expression, with a touch of the 'carnivalesque':

At William Morris how we laughed,
And hairy tweeds and knitted ties:
Pub poets who from tankards quaff'd
Glared up at us with angry eyes –

(SBB 108)

This is not 'deliciously apart' but a near total immersion in group acceptability. Betjeman (despite the University's verdict on him) became his own man because he laughed his way into acceptance among 'gentlemen'. The television Betjeman could retain that guffawing persona to the end. There are worse ways for a man to 'keep' his 'head'.

Summoned by Bells is memento, self-advertisement, and anthem for male youth. It constitutes the blank verse mini-epic of a sensitive and clever man, who invented himself in the teeth of parental, educational, and commercial pressure. It, too, represents a Joycean 'Welcome, O Life!', for all the occasional self-pity, and a forging of the 'conscience of my race' – where 'conscience' has its French sense of consciousness, awareness, and openness to being. And its final voice is made out of a dialogic chumminess:

'Cheer up! You're looking like a soul in hell.
Here's some Amontillado.'

(SBB 110)

However caricatural now, that was the kind of male, officer voice that helped carry Britain through the darkest days of the Second World War, especially at the time when the island stood alone against unleashed evil on the continent of Europe. It represents a kind of masculinity worth cherishing and learning from. Beyond the middle-class intonations, it has the ring of comradeship in courageous survival. So too the coda: the door of Gabbitas Thring's agency hailed with 'welcome'. Here is stoical irony – not quite 'stiff upper lip', but companionably gutsy. It's where the poem has always been heading – a man, my son: a Betjeman, and a *gentleman*.[9]

35

3

The Last of England

Dear old, bloody old England
Of telegraph poles and tin,
Seemingly so indifferent
And with so little soul to win.
What sort of church, I wonder?
The path is a grassy mat,
And grass is drowning the headstones
Sloping this way and that.

(CP 141)

These lines from 'A Lincolnshire Church' come from the 1948
collection *Selected Poems*. The poem represents quintessential
Betjeman, as generally perceived. In thundery weather, the
protagonist (both architectural connoisseur and spiritual
penitent) approaches the church – surrounded by a 'sprinkle
of villas', where a woman stands (smoking, and resentful of
Americans). He enters, assesses the interior detailing, ponders
on the God who inspired the building, and kneels to pray for
forgiveness. The social moment is exact. Power has passed from
the UK to the USA, 'Austerity' lurks as the 'wireless croons',
slacks are in fashion, and telegraph poles hedge about the dire
church restoration of 'eighteen-eighty-eight'. However, the
church ('Middle Pointed') stands for an Englishness far older
than the British Empire, rooted in Christian belief and in the
specifics of a particular locality: 'the wide green marsh'. There is
a 'postmodern' feel to this sponsorship of marginal particularity.
And there is a 'postcolonial' resonance in the poem's surprise
conclusion. For in 'lowering sunlight' stands an 'Indian
Christian priest'. The speaker speculates on the priest's journey
(spiritual as well as geographical) to this time, this place. The
poem affirms him as a friend of God. As the *Bhagavad-Gita* is
woven into the deliberate Anglicizing of the 'American master's'

36

Four Quartets, so the 'lighted East' is here made emblematic of an immigrant pilgrim. Betjeman here shows himself to be an early poet of multiculturalism.

It is possible that 'A Lincolnshire Church' is playing off Eliot's 'Little Gidding'; but it is equally possible that Eliot's fourth section of *Four Quartets* may relate back to Betjeman's earlier 'Exeter' or 'Holy Trinity, Sloane Street'. At any rate, the Second World War helped consolidate an enduring sense of Englishness (opposed to a Europe overrun by Communism and Fascism alike), and the Anglican Church becomes a central signifier. And, in this, Betjeman's kind of poem also anticipates the mode and style of much 'Movement' poetry (set against, for example, Dylan Thomas's imputed 'Celtic' excess). It is known that the leading 'Movement' poet, Philip Larkin, admired Betjeman's work; yet Larkin's poetic contribution is typically described in terms of a Hardy–Yeats polarity ('empiricism' and/or symbolism). However, two of Larkin's best-known earlier poems, 'Church Going' and 'An Arundel Tomb', surely owe more to Betjeman precedents than to anything in the bards of 'Wessex' or the 'Irishry'. 'Church Going', in particular, replicates fairly exactly the Betjeman narrative of entering, interior description, and reflective commentary, even if Larkin's bicycling Mr Bean is self-confessedly ignorant about church architecture. In the Larkin *œuvre,* 'Dear old, bloody old England' will eventually resolve into: 'And that will be England gone'.[1] Betjeman's verdict is never that negative.

In fact, the poet's England, though sometimes nostalgic, is built up in acknowledgement of changes that complicate rather than destroy. The poet himself, after all, was complicit in a contemporary marketing of self-perpetuating Englishness. As Leena Kore Shröder has pointed out,[2] he contributed to Shell slogans such as 'The Severn bores but Shell exhilarates' or 'Land's End but Shell goes on forever'. In 'Dorset', too, Thomas Hardy's Englishness becomes litanized in terms, almost, of commercial brand names: 'Rime Intrinsica, Fontmell Magna, Sturminster Newton and Melbury Bubb' (*CP* 31) – a 'heritage' tour where one could imagine the sale of 'Sturminster Newton Water' or 'Melbury Bubb Cheddar'. Betjeman masterminded the 'Shell Guides' to English counties in the mid-1930s, and he wrote the first two volumes – *Cornwall* and *Devon.* A 'Georgeois' innocent he was not – topography-in-depth was a rhetorical device to get as many of the populace as possible into private cars, purchasing Shell products, and thus revolutionizing the 'habitus'[3] of traditional England. In a similar way, the defender of Victorian Gothic architecture was also a modernist associate of Frederick Etchells (one of the original Vorticists), Nikolaus Pevsner (author of *Pioneers of Modern Design*) and Lazlo Moholy-Nagy (the visionary of modernist photography). Further, as an Oxford friend of W. H. Auden (who was to edit Betjeman's work in America) and a later dining companion of T. S. Eliot, the poet was at the centre of mature English modernism, if not quite of it. Like Eliot, he tried to hold innovation and tradition in balance – the full 'consort'. But he was less interested in theorizing about art than in recognizing it, practising it, and fitting it into the overall, and longer, English scene. His sense of that larger England was spelled out in a wartime broadcast on the BBC Home Service:

> For me, at any rate, England stands for the Church of England, eccentric incumbents, oil-lit churches, Women's Institutes, modest village inns, arguments about cow parsley on the altar, the noise of mowing machines on Saturday afternoons, local newspapers, local auctions, the poetry of Tennyson, Crabbe, Hardy and Matthew Arnold, local concerts, a visit to the cinema... (*LT* 323)

Betjeman was plain about what he disliked in contemporary England – jerry-building, standardization, ugliness, and greed. This is evident in his poem 'Slough' – a piece powerful enough to have stung local poets, of late, into mouthing alternative ripostes on television. Here is Betjeman:

> Those air-conditioned, bright canteens,
> Tinned fruit, tinned meat, tinned milk, tinned beans
> Tinned minds, tinned breath.
>
> . . . . . .
>
> And get that man with double chin
> Who'll always cheat and always win...

> (*CP* 20)

As vehemently as Ezra Pound in the 'Hell Cantos', Betjeman insists on the *infernal* nature of a type of modernity he pins on the particular town. His alternative is less Romantic than environmentally 'Green':

To get it ready for the plough.
The cabbages are coming now;
The earth exhales.

(CP 21)

The technique is bold polarization – with astringent jibes at more innocent things such as radio, 'Tudor' bars, 'peroxide hair', or nail painting. If there are traces of 'old fogy' grudge in this, it is not on behalf of antiquarian 'heritage' but in the cause of a beneficent continuity – 'grass to graze the cow'. It is Jeffersonian as much as Burkean, and surely William Blake (everyone's rent-a-radical) would have approved the sentiment. Betjeman's verse, too, seeks to affirm 'England's green and pleasant land'.

Certainly his 'Essex' constitutes a place-myth quite different from the cliché-*locale* of 'Essex girls'. It evokes a River Lea environment which neither 'railway track' nor Ford's of Dagenham can permanently obliterate:

Where steepest thatch is sunk in flowers
And out of elm and sycamore
Rise flinty fifteenth-century towers.

(CP 159)

It is typical of this socially savvy writer that the poem is conjured out of the pages of a 'colour-plate book'. Outdated rhetoric ('the vagrant visitor erstwhile') is contrasted with realistic diction and still-contemporaneous scenarios: the 'half-land' of 'football clubs'. The poet seems set on superimposing Housman over Edward Thomas to effect a land of lost delight, despite community changes. Essex Englishness remains: an 'uneventful countryside' (CP 158). The narrative of loss in Betjeman (as later in Larkin) serves, in fact, to confirm what it seems to deny. As Robert Colls has quite recently observed, Englishness becomes *re*produced. And the poet's strong contribution to the renewal of national myth is to 'encase' his fine topographical sense in the highly 'native' quatrain:

Like streams the little by-roads run
Through oats and barley round a hill
To where blue willows catch the sun
By some white weather-boarded mill.

(CP 158)

39

That's how it is: Reader, I drive and walk around here.

In the 'New Social Geography' of the 1990s, the idea of place-myth looms large – that is, the cultural idea of places as opposed to geomorphological givens or economic functions. For instance, C. Kern writes in *Place/Culture/Representation*: 'Since the creation of meaning is a distinctly human activity, the turn to culture in the construction of geographical knowledge becomes understandable, for a culture signifies the characteristically human capacity to shape and share meaning.'[4] In *Places on the Margin*, Rob Shields comments that the 'meaning of particular places is a compendium of intersubjective and cultural interpretations over time'.[5] In his contribution to *Maps of Meaning*, Derek Gregory asserts: 'concepts of place, space and landscape have become central to some of the most exciting developments across the whole field of humanities and social sciences';[6] in *Landscape, Politics and Perspectives*, Julian Thomas declares: 'the landscape as a whole comes to be seen as a continuous record of human behaviour, co-varying with ecological conditions';[7] in *Emancipating Space: Geography, Architecture, and Urban Design*, Ross King translates Michel Foucault's idea of 'heterotopia' as 'the actually lived and socially created spaces of life' and evokes 'respect for context – for the pre-existing world of values and memories'.[8] The point of the above listing of titles and quotations is to emphasize the prophetic aspect of Betjeman's topographical sense: what today excites social geographers had been at the heart of the poet's vision (and campaign) from the 1930s – 'Croydon', 'Distant View of a Provincial Town', 'Upper Lambourne', 'South London Sketch, 1944', 'Harrow-on-the-Hill', 'Middlesex', 'Inland Waterway' ...

In his book *England and Englishness*,[9] John Lucas has shown how politically contested the idea of Englishness has been over some three hundred years. And where, say, Tony Harrison or Peter Reading are pitted against Philip Larkin or Andrew Motion that contestation remains well into the contemporary scene. Betjeman's construction of Englishness was less preoccupied with politics (as such) than with social history. It owns to an 'other' ('Ireland with Emily') but is less interested in overall nationhood than in discrete ('marginal') place-myths. Indeed, his dissenting approach to national mythology is well exemplified in 'In Westminster Abbey' – published in *Old Lights* (1940), at the height of England's extremist national crisis:

Think of what our Nation stands for,
  Books from Boots' and country lanes,
Free speech, free passes, class distinction,
  Democracy and proper drains.
Lord, put beneath Thy special care
One-eighty-nine Cadogan Square.

(CP 74)

This 'lady's' satirized prayer embraces 'gallant blacks' and German women, but it is more concerned to protect 'the whites', her own shares, and to condone her 'luncheon date'. With the might of the Wehrmacht less than thirty miles from fortress England, teddy bear John has the *insouciance* to mock the kind of middle-class mentality that most of the world would see as Englishness itself. Betjeman's England is, even *in extremis*, a mind zone where solidarity comes yoked to irony:

I will labour for Thy Kingdom,
  Help our lads to win the war,
Send white feathers to the cowards
  Join the Women's Army Corps...

(CP 75)

This kind of wry 'poeticity' (Richard Rorty's word) was worth fighting for – against political ideology of any colour.

Betjeman's televised commentary 'Metroland' demonstrates how his conception of England was a matter of ongoing negotiation rather than any notional fixity. The tone of social celebration is more pronounced than the echo of nostalgia:

Metroland: the creation of the Metropolitan Railway which, as you know, was the first steam underground in the world. In the tunnels, the smell of sulphur was awful. When I was a boy, 'live in Metroland' was the slogan. It meant getting out of the tunnels, into the country... Bucks, Herts and Middlesex yielded to Metroland, and city men for breakfast on the fast train to London town..

Onwards, onwards, north of the border down Hertfordshire way. The Croxley Green Revels, a tradition that stretches back to nineteen-fifty-two. For pageantry is deep in all our hearts and this, for many a girl, is her greatest day...

[Retiring Queen]: 'I now crown you queen of the Revellers, Croxley Green nineteen-seventy-two.'[10]

There is a sublime dottiness in this encomium, akin to both

41

Virginia Woolf's *Between the Acts* and Stevie Smith's poetic quirkiness. It provides a way of nurturing an ongoing nationality that, even in its imperial heyday, contained a rich leaven of the absurd (Edward Lear, Lewis Carroll, Richard Dadd, Gilbert and Sullivan).

And Metroland has survived into postmodern times. Here, for instance, is early Derek Jarman (1963):

> City waiting as the mist rolls back from the hill, then far distant the sun slants sky parts. It's 8 o'clock today.
>
> Fast down the street to catch the train passing those performing the daily ritual for the last few times. There's Annie ... Her dress and furs are faded and have the preserved quality of glass mortuaries which hold the withered remains of flowers to remind us flowers grew in the old days as now ...
>
> > Round the corner
> > over the bridge
> > down the steps –
> > ticket-smile-and good morning.[11]

Jarman's *Modern Nature* (1991) takes up and develops what was begun here. Both have a touch of Betjeman about them.

Metroland is typically represented in a poem like 'Middlesex' – even though 'Metro' is now 'the tube':

> > Gaily into Ruislip Gardens
> > Runs the red electric train,
> > With a thousand Ta's and Pardon's
> > Daintily alights Elaine ...
> >
> > .   .   .   .   .
> >
> > Out into the outskirt's edges
> > Where a few surviving hedges
> > Keep alive our lost Elysium – rural Middlesex again.
>
> (CP 163)

There is a canny feel for poetic sound here: 'red electric'; 'alights Elaine'; 'lost Elysium'. Such subtleties help 'encase' the theme of change yet also, again, reinforce a sense of continuity. Elaine may be a 'bobby-soxer', but the garden she 'gains' (' – father's hobby – ') serves in a way to connect the house she lives in with the 'hayfields' and 'mayfields' and, indeed, the 'market gardens tidy'. That postmodern phenomenon, the Garden Centre, is yet to come. Yet both market garden and Garden Centre still refer back to the 'lost Elysium' the poem evokes – and help recycle it. In this sense, place-myth may also be compounded of some millions of discrete 'paradises' – suburban gardens backing a home where a one-time Elaine (Tennysonian in name) might, later, be munching her 'sandwich-supper' while watching John Betjeman enthuse on television about the tree-lines at Sherborne or the cricket field at Sidmouth. The 1990s equivalent, in fact, might be a gardening programme or a feature on landscape heritage itself: misty elm, twisting footpaths, and 'cedar-shaped palings'. The 'outskirt's edges' become as much semiotic as geographical boundaries in contemporary Wembley, Northolt, or Greenford. Betjeman's poem mythologizes the process by which this happens. 'History is now and England' – but an Englishness reworked as the 'screen' becomes another scene.

What, then, *is* Betjeman's Englishness (beyond specific localities) – what is it that changes, becomes endangered yet survives? It is not just about 'Women's Institutes, modest village inns', and so on, but centres on a conflictual, ongoing dance of development where satiric critique plays its part:

> Let's say good-bye to hedges
> And roads with grassy edges
> And winding country lanes;
> Let all things travel faster
> Where motor-car is master
> Till only Speed remains.

> ('Inexpensive Progress', (CP 286))

Betjeman's lifelong concern for a beneficent 'habitus' ('hedges', 'edges', 'lanes') constitutes a postmodern environmentalism beyond the political rhetoric of 'the white heat of technology', 'the creation of wealth', or 'modernization'. It is not so much that he is against 'Speed' (he himself enjoyed fast driving), but that he is against any technocratic idolatry that destroys all balance and beauty:

> When all our roads are lighted
> By concrete monsters sited
>
> .   .   .   .   .   .
>
> We'll know that we are dead.

> (CP 287)

Englishness, for the poet, is an ongoing *culture* – something that needs to be nurtured, defended from excess, and constantly renewed. Inevitably, the imagery is 'organic' (as against the mechanization of modernity), stressing maturation, feedback controls, and a future orientation. In terms of 'Gaia', Betjeman's vision is for overall balance, beyond the lifespan of any human individual: in 'Fruit' (*CP* 337), he is content to feel that 'next year's bloom' might live longer than himself. For Betjeman, Englishness is, simply, a form of sanity.

Two later poems, 'Harvest Hymn' and 'Meditation on the A30' demonstrate the poet's application of a 'wise' Englishness to specifically contemporary issues. The first poem promotes environmentalism, the second condemns what is now called 'road rage'. 'Harvest Hymn' is very much in the spirit of Rachel Carson's *Silent Spring* (1962), yet it reflects Betjeman's emphasis since the 1930s:

> We spray the fields and scatter
> The poison on the ground
> So that no wicked wild flowers
> Upon our farm be found.

> (*CP* 284)

John Betjeman is, as it were, the godfather of David Bellamy. The poem utilizes metonymic details – electric fencing, broiler houses, concrete sheds – to set a ruthlessly industrialized form of agriculture against the traditional stewardship of farming: in the brave new world, bungalows 'pay' for 'arable' losses. Ironically 'encase'd in the metre and rhyme of the classic Harvest Festival hymn ('We plough the fields...'), the poem constitutes a radical (rooted) attack on the raw exploitation of the wealth of Creation. It makes an important counter-move in the ecological Battle of Britain – one that 'Friends of the Earth' and similar groupings have explicitly politicized towards the millennium.

'Meditation on the A30' is just as pointed a piece – and one even more prophetic of 1990s perceptions. People, especially men, go lethally, suicidally, crazy in fast cars. Much of the poem is written in the form of internal dialogue (similar to Carol Ann Duffy's contemporary practice): ' "You're barmy or plastered, I'll pass you, you bastard –/I *will* overtake you. I *will*!" ' (*CP* 285). As in Duffy's 'Psychopath', a slightly obvious motivation is set

44

up: 'revenging himself on his wife'. The protagonist objects to his wife's 'temper' and fantasizes about 'a nice blonde on my knee'. Possibly so. But what seems evident is the less emphasized male-versus-male rivalry in the automobile contest. The poem begins: 'A man on his own in a car'. Here Tennyson's Lancelot and de la Mare's 'traveller' combine in a postmodern scenario where masculinity loses its head and puts the blame on a nagging Eve. Yet an important subtext is introduced: 'I only give way to a Jag.' The 'Meditation' is wonderful in its complete inversion of the religious meaning of the term, in its intense encapsulation of obsessionality, and in its deft usage of realistic detail and understatement:

> As he clenches his pipe, his moment is ripe
> And the corner's accepting its kill.

(CP 285)

In such a situation ripeness is, indeed, all. At the present time of writing, this kind of scenario becomes explicit every other month or so: 'pitiful life' sums up the situation.

Aggressive driving is not, of course, a monopoly of the English – and nor is aggressive agricultural practice. The point is that Betjeman's inherent sense of Englishness defines itself against such phenomena, and sees them as a violation of national decency. Raymond Williams might have done a fine job of 'unpacking' the very British sense of decency. Yet perhaps another poem might serve to exemplify it – Betjeman's 'The Hon. Sec.'. For this enacts decency as it quietly eulogizes it in the person of 'Ned'. The opening flag at half-mast sets the mood for an affectionate and generous tribute to a golf-loving man, whose passion is delineated in precise topographical detailing – stream, prospect, upward slope, long fairway... The links is represented as intimately implicated in a specific place and climate, and in the social habits developed within such an English *topos* – cards, whisky, 'scoring'. The golf 'heterotopia' is cannily connected to a very national scenario:

> That garden where he used to stand
> And where the robin waited
> To fly and perch upon his hand
> And feed till it was sated.

(CP 272)

45

There is an endearingly classless quality to this picture (even if the love of birds is more representative of the pigeon-fancying working class than the grouse-shooting aristocracy). The 'epiphany' (for it is surely that) is set against foghorn and rough seas: English culture is a decency of behaviour balanced against the unruly elements on the one hand, the excesses of human nature on the other. Betjeman strikes an Augustan note: 'A gentle guest, a willing host'. And his ending constitutes English understatement at its best:

> It's strange that those we miss the most
> Are those we take for granted

(CP 272)

Betjeman's idiosyncratic version of English 'empiricism' must be seen partly against the sharp Right/Left political opposition-ality of the 1930s. Yet, if the later Sir John can appear as the epitome of one-nation Toryism, it needs to be remembered that the younger Betjeman flirted with Communism, and that he was friends with Anthony Blunt, Tom Driberg, and Clement Attlee. In fact, his overall poetic *œuvre* does not sit easily within the parameters of any overt politics. In particular, it shows no interest in 'isms', and is surely too individualistic to be regarded as political except in environmental and communitarian terms. But throughout it is intensely social. And it consistently deals with social 'structures of feeling', as expressed in tone of voice, visual detailing, and modes of social behaviour that some might wish to relate to political stratifications. But he was no admirer of middle-class Bloomsbury ('physically and mentally cob-webbed men and women', as his friend Robert Byron put it),[12] and his sense of 'Civilization' was by no means limited to the abstracted artefacts of Aestheticism: 'For architecture means not a house, nor a single building or a church but our surroundings, not a town or a street, but our whole over-populated island ...'.[13] In this he was 'one of us' in Conrad's sense (not Baroness Thatcher's). His Englishness consists in an affable, shared, ongoing continuity where choices between beauty and ugliness, coercion and freedom, must constantly be made. In short, he took sides on social issues – not in political terms.

The tendency in English social life that Betjeman most disliked is encapsulated in 'The Town Clerk's Views' – an attitude as characteristic of a kind of Conservatism as much as a type of Labourism. The satirized voice is that of a systematic Utilitarianism:

'In a few years this country will be looking
As uniform and tasty as its cooking.
Hamlets which fail to pass the planners' test
Will be demolished. We'll rebuild the rest
To look like Welwyn mixed with Middle West.

. . . .

And ev'ry old cathedral that you enter
By then will be an Area Culture Centre.

(CP 146)

This is from *Selected Poems* (1948), and it is remarkably canny about prospective social changes shortly to come – the rise of the 'planner', country-life 'rationalization', 'heritage' as sanitized packaging. The Clerk (with 'bye-laws busy in his head') advocates that Dorset be merged with 'Hants' (in fact, Bourne-mouth – 'looking up' – eventually became incorporated into a larger Dorset); Cambridge, accused of 'living in the past', has since become the brain centre of 'Silicon Fen'; and, while Devon and Cornwall have not so far been designated 'South-West Area 1 and 2', there is now a University of the West of England. The idea of planning is, throughout, implicated in notions of the uselessness of old ways (Kentish hopland on one hand, King's College Cambridge on the other). For the bureaucratic mind, 'rationalization' makes things 'beauteous' – a significant lapse from the word 'beautiful'. The inherent social lust for power is lampooned as deftly as it is tediously elaborated throughout the many theoretical tomes of Michel Foucault.

'Huxley Hall' (playing Aldous Huxley's *Brave New World* against Tennyson's two 'Locksley Hall' poems in what has since become Glyn Maxwell terrain) focuses the same satiric intent on a certain Garden City. This is a didactic piece, where the world view of Saint Augustine is pitted against the modernizing of such as Ebenezer Howard and George Bernard Shaw. There may be more than one model for this 'bright, hygienic hell', but for a local dweller it sounds very contemporary Essex–Herts 'New Town':

While outside the carefree children sported in the summer haze
And released their inhibitions in a hundred different ways.

She who eats her greasy crumpets snugly in the inglenook
Of some birch-enshrouded homestead, dropping butter on her
   book...

(CP 160)

Betjeman is, I think, unusually (and unnecessarily) Manichean
in this poem – 'Comrades' versus Christians, as it were. If Barry
has smashed Shirley's dolly, he is likely to get at least an earful,
whether the parent is either a 'stout free-thinker' or a muscular
Christian. And, if we are 'born in Sin', that makes intelligent
instruction about 'Sex and Civics' all the more important. The
spokesperson's 'deep depression' seems more relevant here
than place-myth as emblem of moral vacuity. Perhaps the
'vegetarian dinner' and lime-juice (lacking in gin?) are the real
source of this unwonted Malvolio mood. After all, 'outside the
lightsome poplars flanked the rose-beds in the square' – not a
bad locale in which to traverse the 'seeming accident of Time'.
Betjeman, one feels, protests too much.

'The Costa Blanca' (1974) cunningly pits contemporary
fantasies of Mediterranean escape against an ingrained Englishness. The poem sets up a rather naughty gender contrast: 'SHE'
all for 'the perfect site beside the shore'; 'HE' hankering after
'our Esher lawn'. The Spanish landowner/developer is seen
alternately as Godsend and crook in the two parallel sonnets.
Betjeman is again acute in showing how landscape and desire,
place and myth, are central to human motivation – and thus
may act divisively when *topos* fails to match mythology. The
poem is also centred on a highly contemporary phenomenon –
the crucial era of retirement in an increasingly long-living
Western world. A couple's life savings become invested in an
idea of the Good Life, 'our Casa'. There is a time lapse between
the two utterances – before and after the move is made: the male
voice is placed as 'five years later'. The request to borrow the
Mail in the absence of the *Telegraph* is a nice piece of social
observation. If the husband is to be believed, the couple are
stuck on a 'tideless, tourist-littered' shore, with no proper water
supply, a sharp climb back home, and scorpions in the bath – so
much for 'Casa Kenilworth'. This remains of the moment:
television travel shows routinely feature the annoyance of

disillusioned holiday-makers – who at least can return home. Betjeman is surely one of the earliest poets to make 'Golden Years' fantasy an important feature of contemporary English life.

However, overall, Betjeman's vision of continuing Englishness is enduringly positive – and his role as Poet Laureate became a just confirmation of this. It is worth looking, then, at an 'official' poem, 'Inland Waterway' (1974), when the Queen Mother presided at the 'opening of the Upper Avon at Stratford'. Much laureate poetry tends to be wooden or stilted, but Betjeman drew on his feel for the simple couplet to build up an appropriate cameo of English place-myth. He pulls out familiar, but effective, stops:

> The meadows which the youthful Shakespeare knew
> Are left behind, and, sliding into view,
> Come reaches of the Avon, mile on mile,
> Church, farm and mill and lover-leaned-on stile...

> (CP 338)

This is 'democratic' in that it speaks in tones that Middle England can respond to. In a country where messing about in boats, on both rivers and canals, is a popular pastime, Betjeman acclaims the union of the Avon and Severn (both highly evocative waterways) and conjures up a 'sweet'ness that is English decency at ease. In addressing Majesty, long-term history is added to topographic particularity. The poet, in fact, was reformative in certain ways, but scarcely iconoclastic: nor was he under the illusion that an *avant-garde* was leading grand armies anywhere. He utilizes decorum to reaffirm traditional English priorities: nation, freedom, the sea.

John Betjeman, with his simple diction and sentiments, and his place-myth scenarios, is the quintessential 'contemporary' poet of core Englishness. He has almost nothing to say about Empire (or its loss), 'Great Britain', or some Blakean 'Albion' – but nor does he overemphasize marginal grot as Tony Harrison or Peter Reading could be said to do. For him, 'Inglan' is not a 'Bitch',[14] since he speaks for a Middle England that goes on, mildly, irrespective of the political passions of the intelligentsia or the party in power. Betjeman's career spanned the biggest real threat to England and Englishness since the Armada (1940

49

and all that). What did he make of it? 'Invasion Exercise on the Poultry Farm' begins:

> Softly croons the radiogram, loudly hoot the owls,
> Judy gives the door a slam and goes to feed the fowls.
> Marty rolls a Craven A around her ruby lips
> And runs her yellow fingers down her corduroyed hips...

> (CP 102)

Englishness finally becomes a sane ordinariness of behaviour – if always on the verge of silliness. Away from occupied and theory-struck Paris, in the hazardous land of the free, Betjeman, in the early 1940s, was setting a precedent for much mainstream English poetry to come: 'Are you still taller than sycamores, gallant Victorian spire?' ('Before Invasion, 1940' (CP 97)). No 'outsider', perhaps, understands core Englishness like a sensitive Irishman. What Seamus Heaney writes of Larkin in his lovely essay 'Englands of the Mind' is even truer of Betjeman – Larkin's real forerunner: 'an England of customs and institutions, industrial and domestic, but also an England whose pastoral hinterland is threatened by the very success of those institutions. Houses and roads and factories mean that a certain England is 'Going, Going...'.[15] But not gone: Englishness is not up for auction – to anyone. It endures and flourishes by challenge and response: 'Still heavy with may, and the sky ready to fall...' ('Before Invasion, 1940' (CP 97)). *That* sky was full of falling bombs; but the heart of England fought back – and prevailed. Betjeman was the inevitable laureate of that kind of England.

4

In Praise of Folly

TO GOD'S
GLORY
&
THE HONOR OF
THE
CHURCH OF
ENGLAND
1782

The above inscription, on boards suspended from the roof of a parish church in Somerton, Somerset, 'served...as an inspiration towards' Betjeman's writing of *English Parish Churches* (BB 172). His introduction to the book begins: 'To atheists, inadequately developed building sites...' (BB 172) – a sentiment developed in his own way by Philip Larkin in parts of 'Church Going'. Yet arguments on behalf of atheism, agnosticism, or, indeed, monotheism miss Betjeman's key religious perception: that Anglican Christianity is less about either philosophy or theology than about a sacred *caritas* revealed in hallowed places and buildings, consecrated customs and rituals, dedicated music making, flower arranging, days of special observance or celebration, and reverence for time-honoured 'petits récits'[1] – most particularly from the Bible and Prayer Book. Betjeman's religious genius is to convey this yet, *in extremis*, to question its adequacy:

> I, kneeling, thought the Lord was there.
> Now, lying in the gathering mist
> I know that Lord did not exist;
> Now, lest this "I" should cease to be,
> Come, real Lord, come quick to me.

> ('Before the Anaesthetic...', (CP 107))

Here the poet expresses the essence of any honest religious feeling – the gulf between socialized forms of belief and faith-in-itself, and the unworthiness of the believer. There is surely no reason to endorse Betjeman's sense of personal inadequacy – it is those who lack such who are preposterous (and often dangerous). The poet's profound sense of limitations precisely inspires his genuine virtues – tolerance, humour, and generosity of spirit.

In this, Betjeman's represented Christianity is less an idiosyncratic throwback than a prophetic intimation of a Double Millennium *devotio postmoderna*. His religious poetry, I suggest, has less in common with ecclesiastical 'radical orthodoxy'[2] than with Erasmus's ecumenically forward-looking *In Praise of Folly*. A recent commentary on Erasmus's text, in Patrick Grant's *Literature and Personal Values*, has considerable relevance to the poet's work:

> Erasmus does not consistently succeed in masking his own moralising intent when Folly speaks, so that wit and irony spill over into straightforward social commentary...Erasmus...is free to take such lighthearted, elegant pleasure in Folly, precisely because he believes something clear and certain. For practical purposes he was prepared to admit a consensus that he called 'philosophia Christi', a kind of openness to the plain teachings of Christ in the spirit of shared, common truth...Erasmus singles out the hidebound, pedantic logicians for distorting these generally-accepted Christian truths by obscurantist games, elitist institutions and sterile word-mongering.[3]

The satirical Betjeman (a very canny man, who nevertheless failed in academic 'Divinity') is always against 'obscurantist games' – whether in theological systems, scientistic theories-of-everything, or district-planners' totalitarian social engineering. What he stood for was Christian 'poeticity' rooted in minimalist, but firm, religious conviction: 'behind all the ritual and everything like that, the one fundamental thing is that Christ was God. And it's very hard to believe...But if you can believe it, it gives some point to everything and really I don't think life would be worth living if it weren't true.'[4] Elsewhere, he also periodized his faith as a mode of 'salvation' against Fascism on the one hand, Marxism on the other. But the core remained beyond the political polarities of the 1930s: a consensual 'philosophia Christi'. In 'Christmas' this is expressed in 'Catholic' but non-dogmatic terms:

> That God was Man in Palestine
> And lives to-day in Bread and Wine.

(*CP* 154)

'Hymn' is the second item in Betjeman's *Collected Poems*, and it helps indicate how faith and 'Folly' go together. The overall tone is humorous irony:

> Sing on, with hymns uproarious,
> Ye humble and aloof,
> Look up! And oh how glorious
> He has restored the roof!

(*CP* 4)

Set to the tune of 'The Church's One Foundation', a satirical scenario is outlined concerning the restorational zeal of the late Victorians' tasteless 'modernizing' (removing 'ancient wood-work', the old pews, and the traditional aisle). The new architectural ideas are expressed in terms of brass, baize, pine, marble, and garish stained glass. Socially exact (as one expects of Betjeman), much of the humour derives from the hymnal convention of 'praise-tone', adapted here to somewhat banal detailing – a technique that in Jules Laforgue or early Eliot would be termed 'Romantic irony'. Here it is used with proto-postmodern 'ironism':[5] 'Thou varnishéd pitch-pine!' (*CP* 3). And, of course, the absurdist tone, here, reflects the 'outside' view of religious devotion channelled into such peculiarities as seat arrangements, weather proofing, or general interior decoration: the more so in that yesterday's 'improvements' may become tomorrow's 'ghastly good taste': 'To pave the sweet transition/He gave th'encaustic tile' (*CP* 3). Yet 'Folly' may be the earnest of enduring faith, for, whatever the nature of the 'Restoration', the aim is to renew the 'story' as times change. There is a peculiarly Christian quality in this in so far as *Kerygma* (the message) is about change, conversion, and renewal. So, despite its comicality, 'Hymn' oddly honours 'the sweet transition'. The very intertextual nature of the poem – 'one foundation' to 'Restoration' – acknowledges shared continuity. A 'lighthearted, elegant pleasure' (as Grant writes of Erasmus) is of the essence of any 'philosophia Christi' – hymns, ancient or modern, attest to a divine dimension to what Milan Kundera has beautifully termed 'the unbearable lightness of being'.

53

As in Erasmus, 'Folly' makes for tolerance. Betjeman, the High Church Anglican, is nowhere more himself than when savouring contrastive religious experience – 'Revival ran along the hedge/ And made my spirit whole...'. 'Undenominational' (*CP* 28), like 'A Lincolnshire Church', may well have set a precedent for later church or chapel poems – not only Larkin's 'Church Going' or Michèle Roberts's 'The Return' but also Ted Hughes's jaundiced 'Mount Zion' or R. S. Thomas's empathetic 'The Chapel' ('narrow but saved/in a way men are not now'). But where even Thomas's stance is distanced from the 'conventicle', it is typical that Betjeman is able to convey the place and the experience from within – the shaking lamp-brackets a fine metonymic signifier of nonconformist fervour. It shows the connoisseur of such worship, too, that the chosen hymns are referred to by their tune names: '"Russell Place"... "Saffron Waldron"... "Dorking"'. And while Betjeman, the 'Personality', is known chiefly as a visual expert, the poet also utilizes a keen ear for bells, hymns, and verse cadences. The quatrain form is central here – for it is a staple of hymn writing ('rose...chose' or 'whole...soul'). Although the repeated word 'conventicle' (*illicit* gathering) indicates outsider secrecy, the poet too shares the 'glory', and, though it is undenominational, he characterizes the meeting house as a 'beacon', and 'still the church of God'. Unlike some theological meditations on the matter, Betjeman's ecumenicism is of the heart as well as the head.

'Olney Hymns' is another poem of inter-faith empathy. Where 'An Eighteenth-Century Calvinistic Hymn' (*CP* 8) stresses an emphasis on the idea of Hell, which the poet found horrendous, and 'Calvinistic Evensong' (*CP* 32) focuses on 'aged parish fears', in 'Olney Hymns' the writer who had a good word for the Sandemanians finds even better words for the Calvinistic content of the verses of John Newton and William Cowper. There could scarcely be a stronger endorsement than 'words of Grace which Thou didst choose' (*CP* 78). Olney was, and remains, a town of particular charm and spiritual resonance, and it is through his topographical gift that Betjeman conveys the effect of the hymns: 'the winding Ouse./Pour in my soul...' (*CP* 78). The elm, the river, the 'slopes of clay' give expression to the organic, fluvial, and grounded characteristics of the Olney poets' work. The penultimate line – 'deep...deeper depth' – acknowledges (tactfully) the terrible ending of Cowper's 'The Castaway' ('and whelm'd in deeper gulphs . . .'), and the last line is one of the most limpid and lovely in all Betjeman's *œuvre*: 'This Olney day is any day.' It is surely the case that 'Songs of Praise' is the most popular English religious programme on television, and Betjeman's tuneful, tolerant Christian poetry is of very much the same timbre. It negotiates boundaries with 'the food of love'. (By one of those whims of 'Synchronicity', the 'Songs of Praise' programme broadcast in this week of writing,[6] was introduced by Sir Harry Secombe, included a quotation from R. S. Thomas, and began with a shot of Betjeman's grave at St Enodoc's church.)

'Holy Trinity, Sloane Street MCMVII' (*CP* 47) is at the opposite pole of Betjeman's tolerant range – a 'camp' synaesthesia where Edwardian artiness and religiosity come conjoined: the particular church was Betjeman's favourite for worship in his later years. The poem has a triune structure – *Acolyte, cofirmandus,* and *Priest.* In the first line the 'six white tapers' are reminiscent of the 'nine bean rows' in W. B. Yeats's 'Lake Isle of Innisfree' – Celtic twilight here transmogrified into candle-lit Anglicanism. 'Alma Pater', and 'Saint Oscar' ('lily flowers'), seem to be the presiding presences, and the first verse is transgressively sexualized. The evocation of Cadogan Square in the second verse reminds us of Wilde's arrest at the Cadogan Hotel, even while it evokes wittier Whistler ('you will, Oscar, you will') and the famous painting. The red roses of the third verse again evoke early Yeats, and the whole scene exhales what might be dubbed post-Pre-Raphaelitism. 'Players and painted stage took all my love', wrote the elderly Yeats – and such is true of much of this poem, where the primordial 'stage' is an ecclesiastical building. And yet there is a 'philosophia Christi' within this stagy religiosity – where the suggestive word 'Motherward' leads on to the rather breathless line: 'Wait, restive heart, wait, rounded lips, to pray', and so to the triumphal assertion of divine power at the end. In its sensuous combination of aestheticism and worship, 'Holy Trinity' is a bit like another Yeats poem, 'The Magi' – similarly ceremonious. And it is a rare *caritas* which can savour Sloane Street and Olney to a virtually equal degree.

'Saint Cadoc' expands that *caritas* again; and it is salutary to find gregarious, guffawing 'JB' meditating on the life of a hermit. Of course, the poet's socialite good humour was partly

pose, for, like Eliot's Webster, he was 'much possessed by death'
– as several of his poems show. In this one, a very real fear of
annihilation is slowly palliated by dwelling on St Cadoc's
imagined prayer life – from coffin and fears of Hell to 'death is
now the gentle shore'. As Cadoc seems to breathe God's breath,
so both, in a sense, are embodied in the place – the cell, the cliffs,
the 'thundering bay'. Little sense of the *discipline* of the Saint's
prayer life is given here; simply, the request for vicarious
petitioning is uttered – and granted: 'The Celtic saint has
prayed for me.' The scene is evocatively constructed, from the
rushlighting on the walls and the 'sand and spray' to the rollers
and the shoreline. A slightly Audenesque note is introduced
with reference to the 'archaelogist' – scientific curiosity
intruding on the contemplative life. But the main accent is on
the Saint's oneness with nature and God, his immanent
presentness as well as his past, and hence his efficacy as
intercessor. Betjeman's inherent 'catholicism' is evident in his
sense of the 'communion of saints' – hence his belief that the
prayers of the dead may be 'tongued with fire' beyond the
morbidity of the living. And Cadoc's saintliness is strongly
emphasized by the allusive comparison of his dwelling to a
certain 'lowly cattle stall':

> His little cell was not too small
> For that great Lord who made them all.

> (CP 82)

As in *The Anathemata* of David Jones, Christianity is slyly
represented as 'natural', by its expression in a lived particularity,[7] within a specific topography.

'Christmas', by contrast, somewhat jarringly makes the faith
both contemporaneous and fully socialized:

> Provincial public houses blaze
> And Corporation tramcars clang...

> (CP 153)

Yet there is a Blakean note of 'Innocence' too – 'Become a Child
on earth for me?' -and the insistent questioning in the sixth and
seventh verses is reminiscent of the technique of 'The Tyger' –
hence 'Experience' too. The poem's conclusion is elaborately
prepared for, with a wealth of suggestive metonymy in the

manner of *In Memoriam* – bells, rain, holly, yew, villagers. Yet metonymy, here, is also radically updated and diffused among contrastive place-myths – country, provinces, the metropolis. And Tennyson's pictorial method is further made contemporary by virtually filmic technique – tenements, town hall, London shops, steeples: cutting and panning both. One can imagine, as it were, television shots as the poet moves in and out of frame, volubly directing our attention to details. But all this, and the invocation of casually dressed girls, louts, sleepless children, and Dorchester Hotel residents, is merely a build-up for the penultimate questioning – is the Christmas mythology valid, and did God become incarnate in Jesus? Whatever the pictorial trappings, one belief is affirmed with remarkable clarity and emphasis – in Palestine, God was incarnate in Jesus. That is at the centre of Betjeman's doubting faith. And if necessarily partisan, it is given the force of a 'perennial philosophy'.

'Church of England Thoughts' (*CP* 156–7) constitutes a near-perfect 'objective correlative' for the poet's particularized brand of faith. As the elaborate (five-line) full title makes clear, before we read into the poem, the setting is Betjeman's old college, Magdalen, Oxford, on St Mary Magdalen's Day. Beyond the idea of the Magdalen figure as 'tower', there is none of the Marian mythologization so richly described in Susan Haskins's *Mary Magdalen* (1993). One source of Betjeman's reflections is given in the section 'BELLS' in the Introduction to *English Parish Churches* about bell ringing (or 'the exercise'): 'It is a classless folk art which has survived in the church despite all arguments about doctrine and the diminution of congregations' (*BB* 177). Beyond the Linnaean look of the flower-beds, Magdalen College is seen not as an institution of higher education but as a 'timeless' emblem of English worship ('church bells...are reminders of Eternity' (*BB* 178)). The auditory 'multiplicity' rung from Magdalen Tower becomes set up as *exemplum* of the Anglican Middle Way:

> A church of England sound, it tells
>   Of 'moderate' worship, God and State,
> Where matins congregations go
> Conservative and good and slow
>   To elevations of the plate.

(CP 156)

A 'philosophia Christi' is here rendered local and topographical, such that a marginal garden is made a kind of centralized node in a spiritual web.

The garden where the bells are heard is described as 'a kingdom of its own'. This is a 'grassy kingdom', sweetened by tiger lilies and umbelliferae: as Anglican index (cf. Herbert's Bemerton or Marvell's 'The Garden'), it contrasts strongly with the Romanist imperialism of Augustine's *City of God* (metropolis versus 'Paradise'). The bells not only fill the garden but connect it to the tower and the sky. A lovely, childwise line gives the latter thus: 'And rock the sailing clouds to sleep.' Yet the bells' influence is not confined to the 'good and slow'. Incense-filled churches, humble chapels, and 'pale' country churches are comprehended within the 'changing cadence'. In the penultimate verse it is the bell-ringers' 'exercise' that is stressed: 'the coloured sallies fly/From rugged hands to rafters high' (*CP* 157). The poem ends on a somewhat elegiac note – the onset of later evening made into an epiphany of ecclesiastical decline and fall: 'Before the grassy kingdom fade'. It is a note that will be continuously replayed in poetry and newspapers over the next many years – but without the 'kingdom' vanishing or the bells ceasing. 'Decline and Fall' was a popular motif of what might be called the Oswald Spengler generation (Evelyn Waugh launched a career on the title). But there is also a 'return of the repressed', and a 'classless folk art' is not so easily snuffed out nor an institution that continues to speak for 'Eternity'. It is not the dying fall of the ending that matters most about Betjeman's centrally English poem, but its core vision of ecumenical community: after all, 'we are one body'.

The practical outworking of Betjeman's religious vision is represented in such caring poems as 'House of Rest', 'Devonshire Street W. 1', 'A Child Ill', 'Remorse', or 'The Commander'. The title of the first poem plays off popular euphemisms for death to suggest old age as its own form of arrestment. 'In this small room' makes the old lady's dwelling itself almost a coffin: yet in fact it is tricked out with telling mementoes of a life – wedding photograph, dead husband's tobacco jar, a picture of Lincoln where he was ordained. It appears that this is a 'pastoral' rather than a personal visit, for the narrator does not know the husband's brand of Anglicanism

('"High" or "Low" or "Broad"') and the 'cared-for things' are laid out for him to see. However, the old lady only tenuously inhabits her room, for her mind dwells on the rectory scenario of her past and her lost family life. Is the poet imagining her sons and daughters – or has he been told more than appears? It is not clear yet scarcely matters, for at the centre of the poem is an empathy whereby the woman's life is mentally shared by the narrator during the course of his visit. And, in the same way, the Eucharist bells elicit the old lady's empathy as the 'communion' of ordinary saints:

> The veil between her and her dead
> Dissolves and shows them clear...

> (CP 162)

Rather in the manner of Wordsworth's 'We are Seven', the poem creates a transtemporal spiritual affinity: 'all of them are near' (CP 162).

'Devonshire Street W. 1' exemplifies *caritas* of a different kind – solidarity with a couple blighted by the implications of the medical X-ray photos that the doctor has just given them. The scene is set up in topographical detail – the buildings of that area of London usually known as 'Harley Street'. A fine contrast is created between the solidity of the palisade knob and the short-lived frailty of the man who has received the bad news. And yet, arguably, the poem is more about the fidelity of married love than the awfulness of the potential death sentence. Certainly, the lines move towards this direction. It is not clear whether the wife has gone into the surgery with her husband or has waited in the street: it is probably the latter, since she 'stands timidly by' (CP 177). But, as he is registering the shock (somewhat melodramatically – '"Oh...Londoners!"'), she clasps his hand and suggests they take the tube to save money, thus seeking to bring her husband's mind back to diurnal reality for whatever time he has left. The poem is a finely rendered mini-ballad, piquant but not mawkish. The Christian feeling, here, concerns the frailty of the human 'earthen vessel' and the need (as Auden emended his line) to 'love one another *and* die'.

This sentiment becomes strongly personalized in 'A Child Ill' (CP 180). The poem is poignantly developed in terms of a Neoplatonic polarity between body and soul, and the evocation of a masculine family line – father to son, over three generations. As the poet remembers his father's dying eyes – one soul in fraught dialogue with another – so he looks into the 'questioning' eyes of his ailing, small son. The lines have a simplicity informed by such as Isaac Watts and Blake: 'Oh, little body, do not die.' It is the living body that 'encase's the soul; and this communicates through the eyes without any need of speech. This is a poem about compassion for helplessness, but also about the paternal guilt involved in begetting new life, in a world of suffering, without any satisfactory answers to the deepest questions that offspring voice. There is guilt, too, of a particularly masculine kind, about past failure to give 'full reply' to a stricken father, who 'looked at me and died'. The soul here is a 'light' – but one that, in incarnate terms, can be put out. At the end, the petition addressed to the son's body is redirected to the 'Lord': that the 'Light' may remain 'alight' – a neat word chime. But in the last, repeated line ('Oh, little body...'), a deeply Christian poem remains a profoundly human one. 'Folly', here, resides in the humbling paradox that the soul's immortality comes clothed in all the vulnerability of the flesh.

'Remorse' appears to be another highly personal poem: 'She whom I loved and left is no longer there' (CP 182). The phrase 'loved and left' is a chilling rewriting of Tennyson's 'loved and lost' in In Memoriam – the deep regret recast as a confession of guilt. Somewhat similar in format to 'Death in Leamington' – bedroom, nurse, dead body – 'Remorse' is intensely interiorized and raw. The breath of the dying woman and the resultant corpse ('the shrunken head') are remorselessly realized. The nurse, alone, becomes a distancing device – 'Just one patient the less and little the loss to her', a touch of both Wordsworth and Hardy in the last phrase. Guilt, pain, and incipient loss are all evoked in 'worry and waiting and troublesome doubt'. So they are in the brief meditation on comparative irrelevances that come between persona and the loved one: 'Protestant claims and Catholic'. The self-accusation is direct and uncompromising – 'neglect and unkindness'. It would be impertinent to underline biographical features at work in the poem – and the lines are poetically realized enough to operate as 'objective correlative' for intense personal experience in general. People love each other, and differ: and guilt attends any close death. The narrator would endure again the painful vigil at the death bed if he could emend the past. Yes, the protective reader might respond – but remember Hopkins's 'My own heart let me more have pity on'.

'The Commander' comes to death-in-life in a more Augustan style – urbane, reflective, commemorative:

> I remembered our shared delight in architecture and nature
>   As bicycling we went
> By saffron-spotted palings to crumbling box-pewed churches...
>
> (CP 268)

This is a poem of rich generosity of spirit: 'the greatness of things was in you...'. The 'Commander's' psalmic tag is reiterated: "Lord, I am not high-minded...". Betjeman is able to deploy an eighteenth-century urbanity steeped in appreciative friendship. In this he is not afraid to deploy the 'marginalized' word 'soul', and to trust in its survival after death. In the case of his friend, the soul revealed itself in physical habit – cycling, Quaker silence, Dickens reading, administration, or sharing wine with his family. But the repeated word 'Lord' provides a baseline for this form of religious wisdom – an unpretentious humility ('Dear Lord and Father of mankind/Forgive our foolish ways...'). Betjeman, the High Church ritualist, again shows his ecumenical openness in savouring a contrastive means of Grace.

'Greek Orthodox', dedicated to 'the Reverend T. P. Symonds', is another late poem of friendship and fellowship. It is written in relaxed, urbane couplets of the kind recently deployed in Tony Harrison's 'Cypress and Cedar'. A specific *locale* is evolved with the help of 'Edward Lear':

> Show me the Greece of wrinkled olive boughs
> Above red earth; thin goats, instead of cows,
> Each with its bell; the shallow terraced soil...
>
> (CP 319)

This is not W. B. Yeats's rhetorical and *Symboliste* 'Byzantium', but simply – Greek Orthodox. It is exactly particularized, for all that we are far from 'Betjeman Country'. As the poet writes, 'who knows how old...?' – not a question we would expect to find in the poet's English architectural commentaries. Nevertheless, Betjeman's architectural *feel* is at work: 'The domed interior swallows up the day' – *mots justes*. A playful 'dialogue' with the English vicar is created to sketch the difference between differing religious customs. The Greeks' more casual 'taste' is defended: 'It needs no bureaucratical protection./It is its own perpetual resurrection' (*CP* 320), and there is a sly dig at the pretence of Roman Catholicism to universality – 'the Pope's in Rome'. Betjeman dwells on the specifics of village bells and services, and conveys the popularity and 'naturalness' of the church in its environment of port, village, and sea. Unerringly, the finale homes in on the most arresting feature of such church interiors:

> The Pantocrator's searching eyes of brown,
> With one serene all-comprehending stare...

> (*CP* 320)

The dome interior, so contrastive to the steeple-haunted exteriors of 'Northern' churches, gathers the worshippers – a village-full it seems – in a commanding, but profoundly 'feminine', embrace. 'Philosophia Christi' exists here as 'Holy Wisdom' (Hagia Sophia), beneficent for 'farmer, fisherman and millionaire'.

John Betjeman's Christianity is based, then, on a charitable, humorous and non-dogmatic core faith – the kind of phenomenon implicit in Renaissance scholar M. A. Screech's recent book, *Laughter at the Foot of the Cross*. It subsumes variants of the word 'holy' – wholesome, healing, hale, holistic, whole. The first volume of the poet's letters evidences Betjeman's defensive discomfort when Evelyn Waugh took it on himself to champion Penelope Betjeman's decision for Romanism. Waugh, in fact, threatened teddy bear John with Hell – much as school bullies once kicked the budding poet up his backside. In my view, Betjeman comes out well in this exchange. He could no more adhere to dogmatic theology than to the systematic theories of Marx or Freud. His kind of Anglicanism is similar to Milan Kundera's 'poeticity': 'The novel's wisdom is different from that of philosophy. The novel is born not out of the theoretical spirit but the spirit of humor... The art inspired by God's laughter does not by nature serve ideological attitudes: it contradicts them. Like Penelope, it undoes each night the tapestry that the theologians, philosophers and learned men have woven the day before...'.[8] In Betjeman, humour and wisdom come together as a mode of waiting on God.

Hence, the charge of 'anti-intellectualism' that Tom Paulin has made against the poet[9] rather misses the point, for all that there is truth in it. Maurice Bowra declared that 'Betjeman has a mind of extraordinary originality; there is no one else remotely like him'.[10] But his intelligence resided not in abstract ideas but in a remarkable openness to impressions, thoughts, and insights. In religious terms, he initiates a *devotio postmoderna* of tolerant ecumenicism that is very much in the spirit of the Renaissance *devotio moderna* – a kind of Christian 'back to basics'. In postmodern terms, the problem with classical theology resides precisely in its 'Gutenberg' systematicity – its favouring of *Logos* as web of words over the Word made flesh. Betjeman favours spirit over letter. And his poetry honours the 'Folly' of believing that God became incarnate, hence humans – however unworthy – can partake of something of the divine nature.

Such a belief enabled the poet to face the world and his own deepest fears with a degree of equanimity, and to become spokesperson for a postmodern English 'nonsense' imbued with spiritual sanity. Thus the near-frivolity of some of his collection titles: *Continual Dew; New Bats in Old Belfries; A Few Late Chrysanthemums; A Nip in the Air*. Betjeman never took himself over-seriously (unlike, say, R. S. Thomas). Even at his most cutting, there remains a touch of charitable whimsy:

> It's not their fault they often go
> To Maidenhead...

> ('Slough', (CP 21))

Like some of the sayings of Jesus (from 'motes' to 'beams'), Betjeman's poems use humour to make a point about wholesome living. He is, too, the 'People's Poet' partly because of this. In religious terms, his work is akin to Sara Maitland's feminist Christianity:

> We need jugglers and high-wire artistes – sequinned, sparkling and dancing on the void – if theology is to measure up to the magnificent God whose gambling habits and sleights of hand boggle our simple minds. We need a deeply imaginative meditation on the narratives and symbols of our past if we hope to co-create a

future ... We won't get any of this until the poets are embraced and allowed, encouraged, loved into running all the risks they want.[11]

The risk of 'Folly' – of laughter, populist jingles, and undogmatic faith – is Betjeman's idiosyncratic way of 'bearing witness':

> But I hope the preacher will not think
> It unorthodox and odd
> If I add that I glimpse in 'the Mistress'
> A hint of the Unknown God.
>
> ('Lenten Thoughts of a High Anglican', (CP 311))

Notes

CHAPTER 1.   TO ENCASE IN RHYTHM AND RHYME

1. 'That dear good man, with Prufrock in his head/And Sweeney waiting to be agonised...' (*SBB* 29). The references are to 'The Love Song of J. Alfred Prufrock' (actually completed in 1912 – although not published in England until 1917: 'in his head' as memory, then), and to 'Sweeney Agonistes' (finalized in autumn 1925, but 'Unfinished'). See *The Complete Poems and Plays of T. S. Eliot* (London: Faber & Faber, 1969), 13–17, 115–26). Betjeman may have had other of Eliot's Sweeney poems in mind – for instance 'Sweeney among the Nightingales' (ibid. 56–7): 'The nightingales are singing near/the Convent of the Sacred Heart', for instance, sounds somewhat proto-Betjemanian.
2. A point well made by Leena Kore Shröder in 'Heterotopian Constructions of Englishness in the Work of John Betjeman', *Critical Survey*, 10/2 (1998), 15–34. This unusually original essay has also helped prompt some of my references to Betjeman's involvement in Shell advertising and his construction of 'place-myth', *passim*.
3. I am alluding to Thomas Kuhn's usage of 'paradigm shift' and 'normal science' in his highly influential work *The Structure of Scientific Revolutions* (Chicago: University of Chicago Press, 1962).
4. Wilfred Bion, *Attention and Interpretation* (New York: Jason Aranson, 1983), 122.
5. Michael Rustin, *The Good Society and the Inner World: Psychoanalysis, Politics and Culture* (London: Verso, 1991), 196–7.
6. John Ashbery, 'The Village of Sleep', *London Review of Books*, 5 Feb. 1998, 23.
7. Geoffrey Grigson, 'Hendren-Rhododendron', *The Contrary View* (London: Macmillan, 1974), 8.
8. Antony Easthope, *Poetry as Discourse* (London: Methuen, 1983), 54.
9. Ibid. 77.
10. Quoted from the poet's *Spectator* article of 8 Oct. 1954 in John Press,

John Betjeman (London: Longmans, 1974), 21.

11. Christopher Ricks (ed.), *T. S. Eliot: Inventions of the March Hare, Poems 1909–1917* (New York: Harcourt Brace & Co, 1996).

12. 'Interview' (Dennis Brown talking to Robin Robertson), *Critical Survey*, 10/1 (1998), 107.

13. T. S. Eliot, 'Hamlet' (1919), *Selected Essays* (Faber & Faber, 1958), 145.

14. Susanne Küchler, *Landscape: Politics and Perspectives*, ed. Barbara Bender (Providence, RI, and Oxford: Berg, 1993), 85.

15. Glyn Maxwell, 'Garden City Quatrains', *Rest for the Wicked* (Newcastle upon Tyne: Bloodaxe Books, 1995), 51.

16. Bevis Hillier, *Young Betjeman* (London: John Murray, 1988), 75, and William Plomer, *Contemporary Poets* (London: St James's Press, 1975), 117.

17. Hillier, *Young Betjeman*, 339.

18. Patrick Taylor-Martin, *John Betjeman: His Life and Work* (London: Allen Lane, 1983), 53.

19. Michèle Roberts, 'The Return', quoted here from *The New Poetry*, ed. Michael Hulse, David Kennedy, and David Morley (Newcastle upon Tyne: Bloodaxe Books, 1993), 150.

20. Umberto Eco, 'In Praise of St Thomas', *Travels in Hyperreality*, essays, translated from the Italian by William Weaver (London: Picador, 1987), 258.

21. Antony Easthope, *Poetry and Phantasy* (Cambridge: Cambridge University Press, 1989), 43, 45.

22. See Shröder, 'Heterotopian Constructions of Englishness'.

CHAPTER 2.   A MAN, MY SON

1. 'I thought every German was you./And the language obscene' ('Daddy', Sylvia Plath, *Collected Poems* (London: Faber and Faber, 1981), 223). For Plath's self-consciousness about her Germanicity, see Dennis Brown, *The Poetry of Postmodernity: Anglo/American Encodings* (London: Macmillan; New York: St Martins, 1994), 48–9.

2. Sigmund Freud, *Introductory Lectures on Psychoanalysis*, trans. James Strachey (London: Penguin, 1978), 424.

3. Saint Augustine, *Confessions*, trans. R. S. Pine-Coffin (London: Penguin, 1984), 21.

4. Robert Bly, *Iron John: A Book about Men* (Shaftesbury: Element, 1992), 153.

5. Máirtín Mac An Ghaill (ed.), *Understanding Masculinities* (Buckingham: Open University Press, 1996).

6. British School psychoanalysis has emphasized the practical, therapeutic aspects of the 'talking cure' at the expense of

systematic theorizing. See e.g. Michael Rustin, *The Good Society and the Inner World: Psychoanalysis, Politics and Culture* (London: Verso, 1991), Andrew Samuels, *The Political Psyche* (London and New York: Routledge, 1993), and Robert Young's powerful article 'The Vicissitudes of Transference and Countertransference: The Work of Harold Searles', *Free Associations*, vol. 5, pt. 2, no. 34 (1995).
7. Patrick Grant, *Literature and Personal Values, Spiritual Discourse and the Meaning of Persons*, and *Personalism and the Politics of Culture: Readings in Literature and Religion from the New Testament to the Poetry of Northern Ireland* (London: Macmillan; New York: St Martins, 1992, 1994, 1996).
8. A contemporary's phrase quoted by Bevis Hillier, *Young Betjeman*, 131.
9. I owe this last phrase to a highly perceptive commentary by my former colleague and friend, George Wotton.

CHAPTER 3.   THE LAST OF ENGLAND

1. Philip Larkin, 'Going, Going', *Collected Poems*, ed. with an Introduction by Anthony Thwaite (London: Faber & Faber, 1990), 190.
2. Leena Kore Shröder, 'Heterotopian Constructions of Englishness', 19.
3. A term utilized by Pierre Bourdieu, *Outline of a Theory of Practice*, trans. R. Nice (Cambridge, Mass.: MIT Press, 1977). Rob Shields discusses its meanings in *Places on the Margin: Alternative Geographies of Modernity* (London: Routledge, 1991), 32–8. It seems similar to place-myth, but adds the sense of lived habitation and habit.
4. C. Kern, in *Place/Culture/Representation* (London: Routledge, 1993), 29.
5. Shields, *Places on the Margin*, 25.
6. Peter Jackson (ed.), *Maps of Meaning: An Introduction to Cultural Geography* (London: Routledge, 1992), p. ix.
7. Julian Thomas, *Landscape, Politics and Perspectives*, ed. Barbara Bender (Providence, RI, and Oxford: Berg, 1993), 19.
8. Ross King, *Emancipating Space: Geography, Architecture and Urban Design* (London and New York: The Guilford Press, 1996), 123, 148.
9. John Lucas, *England and Englishness: Ideas of Nationhood in English Poetry 1688–1900* (London: Hogarth Press, 1990).
10. John Betjeman, 'Metroland', 1 of 5 and 3 of 5, *Television Scripts*, transcribed by David Hodges and Vince Russell on 'JB Home Page' website compiled by Steven Phillips, 17 Jan. 1998, Internet. A shorter lineated version is found in *BB* 216–17.

11. Derek Jarman, 'Notes Found on the Body of a BA General Student', *Lucifer: King's College Review* (London) (Lent Term 1963), 21. I was then the editor, Derek the art editor, of *Lucifer*. (Derek's *The Last of England* was published by Constable (London) in 1987; his *England/A Time of Hope* is dated 1981.)
12. Quoted in Bevis Hillier, *Young Betjeman*, 328.
13. Quoted in Bevis Hillier, *John Betjeman: A Life in Pictures* (London: John Murray, 1984), 169.
14. Linton Kwesi Johnson, 'Inglan's a Bitch', here quoted from *The New Poetry*, ed. Michael Hulse, David Kennedy, and David Morley, 187.
15. Seamus Heaney, 'Englands of the Mind', here quoted from *Literature in the Modern World: Critical Essays and Documents*, ed. Dennis Walder (Oxford: Oxford University Press, in association with the Open University, 1990), 257.

CHAPTER 4.   IN PRAISE OF FOLLY

1. Cf. 'I define *postmodern* as incredulity towards metanarratives', and: 'Consider the form of popular sayings, proverbs, and maxims...In their prosody can be recognized the mark of that strange temporalization that jars the golden rule of our knowledge: "never forget"' (Jean-François Lyotard, *The Postmodern Condition: A Report on Knowledge*, trans. Geoff Bennington and Brian Massumi (Manchester: Manchester University Press, 1986), pp. xxiv, 22). Lyotard's book was first published as *La Condition postmoderne: Rapport sur le. savoir* (1979). It was commissioned by the 'Conseil des Universités of the government of Quebec' (back cover). Since the book has been highly influential, it is interesting (in terms of Canadian politics) that it largely updates ideas that Marshall McLuhan had propounded in the 1960s – from the University of Toronto (Ontario). McLuhan was highly influenced by the late views of the English writer and painter Wyndham Lewis.
2. This phrase is apparently used as a slogan by such contemporary theologians as Philip Blond, Gerald Loughlin, John Milbank, Catherine Pickstock, and Graham Ward. See 'Rains for a Famished Land', *Times Literary Supplement*, 10 Apr. 1998, 12–13.
3. Patrick Grant, *Literature and Personal Values* (Basingstoke: Macmillan; New York: St Martin's, 1992), 135.
4. Quoted by Bevis Hillier, *John Betjeman: A Life in Pictures* (London: John Murray, 1984), 187.
5. Cf. 'One of my aims...is to suggest the possibility of a liberal

utopia, one in which ironism, in the relevant sense, is universal' (Richard Rorty, *Contingency, irony and solidarity* (Cambridge: Cambridge University Press, 1989), p. xv).

6. 'Songs of Praise', BBC1, 5.55–6.30 pm, 19 July 1998.
7. The 'postmodern' relevance of this strategy is evident from Edith Wyschogrod, *Saints and Postmodernism: Revisioning Moral Philosophy* (Chicago and London: The University of Chicago Press, 1990), *passim*.
8. Milan Kundera, *The Art of the Novel*, trans. Linda Asher (New York: Grove Press, 1986), 160. The passage is tellingly quoted in Richard Rorty, *Philosophical Papers*, ii. *Essays on Heidegger and Others* (Cambridge: Cambridge University Press, 1991), 73.
9. Tom Paulin, quoted in 'New Views on Betjeman: The Teddy Bear and the Critics', *Listener*, 23 May 1985.
10. Maurice Bowra quoted in Bevis Hillier, *Young Betjeman*, 141.
11. Sara Maitland, *A Big-Enough God: Artful Theology* (London: Mowbray, 1995), 145.

Select Bibliography

WORKS BY JOHN BETJEMAN

Poetry

Mount Zion (London: the James Press, 1931).

Continual Dew: A Little Book of Bourgeois Verse (London: John Murray, 1937).

Old Lights for New Chancels: Verses Topographical and Amatory (London: John Murray, 1940).

New Bats in Old Belfries (London: John Murray, 1945).

Slick, But Not Streamlined: Poems and Pieces Selected and with an Introduction by W. H. Auden (New York: Doubleday, 1947).

Selected Poems: Chosen with a Preface by John Sparrow (London: John Murray, 1948).

A Few Late Chrysanthemums (London: John Murray, 1954).

Poems in the Porch (London: SPCK, 1954).

Collected Poems (London: John Murray, 1958, with later and enlarged editions).

Summoned by Bells (London: John Murray, 1960).

High and Low (London: John Murray, 1966).

Collected Poems: A New and Enlarged Edition with an Introduction by Philip Larkin (Boston: Houghton Mifflin, 1971).

A Nip in the Air (London: John Murray, 1974).

Uncollected Poems, with a Foreword by Bevis Hillier (London: John Murray, 1982).

Collected Poems (enlarged edition; London: John Murray, 1988).

Prose

Ghastly Good Taste (London: Chapman & Hall, 1933).

Cornwall: Illustrated (London: the Architectural Press, 1934).

Devon: A Shell Guide (London: the Architectural Press, 1936).

An Oxford University Chest (London: John Miles, 1938).

Antiquarian Prejudice (London: Hogarth Press, 1939).

Vintage London (London: William Collins, 1942).

English Cities and Small Towns (London: William Collins, 1943).

John Piper (London: Penguin Books, 1944).

Murray's Buckinghamshire Architectural Guide, with John Piper (London: John Murray, 1948).

Murray's Berkshire Architectural Guide, with John Piper (London: John Murray, 1949).

Shropshire: A Shell Guide, with John Piper (London: Faber & Faber, 1951).

First and Last Loves (London: John Murray, 1952).

Collins Guide to English Parish Churches (London: William Collins, 1958).

English Churches, with Basil Clarke (London: Studio Vista, 1964).

The City of London Churches (London: Pitkin Pictorials, 1965).

London's Historic Railway Stations (London: John Murray, 1972).

A Pictorial History of English Architecture (London: John Murray, 1972).

Archie and the Strict Baptists (London: John Murray, 1977).

Coming Home; An Anthology of his Prose, 1920–1977, selected and introduced by Candida Lycett Green (London: Methuen, 1997; paperback edn., London: Vintage, 1988).

John Betjeman: Letters Volume One 1926 to 1951, ed. Candida Lycett Green (London: Methuen, 1994).

John Betjeman: Letters Volume Two 1952 to 1984, ed. Candida Lycett Green (London: Methuen, 1995).

ANTHOLOGY OF JOHN BETJEMAN'S KEY WRITINGS

The Best of Betjeman, selected by John Guest (London: Penguin in association with John Murray, 1978). This includes 'Metroland'.

CRITICAL AND BIOGRAPHICAL STUDIES

Books

A Bibliographical Companion to Betjeman, compiled by Peter Gammond with John Heald (Guildford: The Betjeman Society, 1997).

Brooke, J., *Ronald Firbank and John Betjeman* (London & New York: Longmans, Green, 1963).

Delaney, Frank, *Betjeman Country* (London: Hodder and Stoughton, 1983).

Hillier, Bevis, *John Betjeman: A Life in Pictures* (London: John Murray, 1984).

_____ *Young Betjeman* (London: John Murray, 1988).

Press, John, *John Betjeman* (London: Longmans, 1974).

Stanford, Derek, *John Betjeman: A Study* (London: Neville Spearman, 1961).

Taylor-Martin, Patrick, *John Betjeman: His Life and Work* (London: Allen Lane, 1983).

Articles

Harvey, G.. 'Poetry of Commitment: John Betjeman's Later Writing', *Dalhousie Review*, 56 (1976) 112–24.

Horder, Mervyn, 'Setting John Betjeman to Music', *Contemporary Review*, 265/1542 (July 1994), 39–41.

Hulse, Michael, 'The Laureate Business or the Laureateship in Englishness', *Quadrant*, 29/2 (Sept. 1985), 46–9.

Larkin, Philip, 'It Could Only Happen in England', *Cornhill Magazine*, (Autumn 1971) 1069.

Ruddick, Bill, ' "Some Ruin-Bibber, Randy for Antique": Philip Larkin's Response to the Poetry of John Betjeman', *Critical Quarterly*, 84/4 (Winter 1986), 63–9.

Schröder, Leena Kore, 'Heterotopian Constructions of Englishness in the Work of John Betjeman', *Critical Survey*, 10/2 (1998), 15–34.

Thomas, Peter, 'Reflections on the Collected Poems of John Betjeman', *Western Humanities Review*, 27 (1973) 289–94.

Wilson, Edward, 'Betjeman's Riddle Posts: An Echo of Ninian Comper', *Review of English Studies*, 42/168 (Nov. 1991), 541–50.

FURTHER READING

Armitage, Simon, and Crawford, Robert (eds.), *The Penguin Book of Poetry from Britain and Ireland since 1945* (London: Viking, 1998). See the Introduction.

Blamires, Harry, *Twentieth-Century English Literature* (2nd edn., Basingstoke: Macmillan Education, 1986).

Carpenter, Humphrey, *The Brideshead Generation: Evelyn Waugh and his Friends* (London: Weidenfeld and Nicolson, 1989).

Cunningham, Valentine, *British Writers of the Thirties* (London: Oxford University Press, 1988).

Ford, Boris, (ed.), *The Present* (*The New Pelican Guide to English Literature*), 8; Harmondsworth: Penguin, 1983).

Fraser, G. S. *The Modern Writer and his World* (London: Derek Vershoyle, 1953).

Martin, Graham, and Furbank, P. N. (eds.), *Twentieth Century Poetry: Critical Essays and Documents* (Milton Keynes: Open University Press, 1975).

Morrison, Blake, *The Movement: English Poetry and Fiction of the 1950s* (London: Oxford University Press, 1980).

Powell, Anthony, *Under Review: Further Writings on Writers* (London: Heinemann, 1991).

Press, John, *Rule and Energy: Trends in British Poetry since the Second World War* (London: Oxford University Press, 1963)

Schmidt, Michael, *A Reader's Guide to Fifty Modern British Poets* (London: Heinemann; New York: Barnes & Noble, 1979).

Index

INDEX to COMMENTARY on INDIVIDUAL POEMS

'Henley-on-Thames', 14
'Hertfordshire', 13
'Holy Trinity, Sloane Street', 55
'House of Rest', 58–9
'Huxley Hall', 47–8
'Hymn', 53

'Inexpensive Progress', 43–4
'Inland Waterway', 49
'Invasion Exercise on the Poultry
    Farm', 50
'In Westminster Abbey', 40–1

'Meditation on the A30', 44–5
'Middlesex', 42–3

'Olney Hymns', 54–5

'Remorse', 60–61

'Saint Cadoc', 55–6

'Slough', 38–9
'St. Saviour's, Aberdeen Park,
    Highbury, London, N', 19–20
'Summoned by Bells', 16–17, 22–
    35
'Sunday Afternoon Service in St
    Enodoc Church, Cornwall', 15

'The Arrest of Oscar Wilde at the
    Cadogan Hotel', 12–13
'The Commander', 61
'The Costa Blanca', 48–9
'The Hon. Sec.', 45–6
'The Town Clerk's Views', 46–7
'The Village Inn', 14

'Uffington', 21

'Youth and Age on Beaulieu
    River, Hants', 13

Recent and
Forthcoming Titles
in the
New Series of

WRITERS AND
THEIR WORK

"... this series promises to outshine its own
previously high reputation."
Times Higher Education Supplement

"...will build into a fine multi-volume critical
encyclopaedia of English literature."
Library Review & Reference Review

"...Excellent, informative, readable, and recommended."
NATE News

"written by outstanding contemporary critics,
whose expertise is flavoured by unashamed enthusiasm for
their subjects and the series' diverse aspirations."
Times Educational Supplement

"A useful and timely addition to the ranks of the lit crit and
reviews genre. Written in an accessible and authoritative style."
Library Association Record

RECENT & FORTHCOMING TITLES

RECENT & FORTHCOMING TITLES

TITLES IN PREPARATION

Title	Author
Chinua Achebe	*Nahem Yousaf*
Pat Barker	*Sharon Monteith*
Samuel Beckett	*Keir Elam*
Elizabeth Bowen	*Maud Ellmann*
Charlotte Brontë	*Sally Shuttleworth*
Lord Byron	*Drummond Bone*
Cymbeline	*Peter Swaab*
Daniel Defoe	*Jim Rigney*
Charles Dickens	*Rod Mengham*
Early Modern Sonneteers	*Michael Spiller*
T.S. Eliot	*Colin MacCabe*
Brian Friel	*Geraldine Higgins*
The *Gawain* Poet	*John Burrow*
Ivor Gurney	*John Lucas*
Henry V	*Robert Shaughnessy*
Geoffrey Hill	*Andrew Roberts*
Christopher Isherwood	*Stephen Wade*
Kazuo Ishiguro	*Cynthia Wong*
Ben Jonson	*Anthony Johnson*
John Keats	*Kelvin Everest*
Rudyard Kipling	*Jan Montefiore*
Charles and Mary Lamb	*Michael Baron*
Language Poetry	*Alison Mark*
Malcolm Lowry	*Hugh Stevens*
Macbeth	*Kate McCluskie*
Harold Pinter	*Mark Batty*
Dennis Potter	*Derek Paget*
Religious Poets of the 17th Century	*Helen Wilcox*
Revenge Tragedy	*Janet Clare*
Richard III	*Edward Burns*
Siegfried Sassoon	*Jenny Hartley*
Mary Shelley	*Catherine Sharrock*
Six Modern Feminist Playwrights	*Dimple Godiwala*
Stevie Smith	*Martin Gray*
Muriel Spark	*Brian Cheyette*
Gertrude Stein	*Nicola Shaughnessy*
Laurence Sterne	*Manfred Pfister*
Tom Stoppard	*Nicholas Cadden*
The *Tempest*	*Gordon McMullan*
Tennyson	*Seamus Perry*
Derek Walcott	*Stewart Brown*
John Webster	*Thomas Sorge*
Edith Wharton	*Janet Beer*
Jeanette Winterson	*Margaret Reynolds*
Women Romantic Poets	*Anne Janowitz*
Women's Gothic	*Emma Clery*
Women Writers of the 17th Century	*Ramona Wray*
Women Poets of the Mid 19th Century	*Gill Gregory*
Women Writers of the Late 19th Century	*Gail Cunningham*